STUDIES IN
PROVERBS

HERMAN O. WILSON

SWEET PUBLISHING COMPANY

Austin   Texas 78765

Library of Congress Catalog Card Number: 71-92631
Standard Book Number: 8344-0056-1

Printed in the United States of America

STUDIES IN PROVERBS

CONTENTS

Nothing ever becomes real till it is experienced. Even a Proverb is no Proverb to you till your life has illustrated it.

John Keats

Chapter One

THE REWARDS
OF TRUE WISDOM

Wisdom is the principal thing; therefore get wisdom.
Proverbs 4:7

THE PROVERBS, like other books of the Bible, used to be an important part of a young man's education; but today the terse, pithy sayings of this book are generally neglected in favor of newspaper columns giving advice on the age-old problems of the human heart and the conduct of life.

This ancient book of sage counsel deserves to be better known than it is today, for its warnings, pleadings, and wisdom are as apt and timely now as in grandfather's day or any period of history. Many of the precepts in Proverbs—especially its teachings on self control, child guidance, and concern for the poor—are especially appropriate in this unsettled time.

The Proverbs, generally classified as one of the poetic books of the Old Testament, belong to a broad category known as wisdom literature. This literary genre was once common in the Near East. Its material is drawn from many levels of life and from a wide range of human experience. Although its subject matter is far-reaching, this book is unified by one oft-repeated aim: to reprove the evil in men's lives and to encourage each reader to seek wisdom, truth, and righteousness.

Two main types of wisdom literature are found—the proverbial, consisting of brief, pointed sayings having a didactic purpose, represented by the Proverbs, and philosophical, such as the book of Ecclesiastes and the dramatic dialogues of Job.

7

STUDIES IN PROVERBS

The book of Proverbs is rich in aphorisms, that is, practical advice on a host of subjects, from anger and envy to such topics as training children, caring for property, and avoiding the pitfalls of idleness and adultery. Interspersed among the warnings are strong urgings to work, to practice thrift, to seek honor and a good reputation, and above all to love wisdom and enjoy its rewards. What the book lacks in unity it makes up for in diversity. "Here," in Dryden's fine phrase, though far from its context, "is God's plenty."

The book of Proverbs deals with the conduct of life. No other book in the Old Testament canon resembles the Proverbs in either subject matter or style. All phases of human life and behavior are discussed, as well as man's relation to God. Truth, beauty, and goodness are summed up in the all-important term *wisdom*, and all forms of evil (personal or national) are pictured as folly or disobedience to divine law.

The style of this richly varied and practical book is unique. Although there are thirty-one chapters, each consisting of many verses, there is no clearly discernible continuity in subject matter. Sometimes a chapter (like most of chapter three) may be devoted to a single topic; more often the chapter may contain a wide variety of topics (as chapter twenty-two, for example, in which each verse seems to introduce a new topic).

The typical pattern of the Old Testament proverbs is a couplet consisting of two short sentences which express a single thought:

A good name is rather to be chosen than great riches,
And loving favor rather than silver and gold.   (22:1)

In this pattern the second line usually restates or reinforces the idea of the first line. A second very common pattern uses the second line to reverse or state the opposite of line one:

He that is slow to anger is of great understanding;
But he that is hasty of spirit exalteth folly.

(14:29)

A third variation, in which the second, or second and succeeding lines, complete the thought of the first, is also common:

The eyes of Jehovah are in every place,
Keeping watch upon the evil and the good.
(15:3)

The fear of Jehovah is to hate evil:
Pride, and arrogancy, and the evil way,
And the perverse mouth, do I hate.
(8:13)

Honor Jehovah with thy substance,
And with the first-fruits of all thine increase;
So shall thy barns be filled with plenty,
And thy vats shall overflow with new wine.

(3:9, 10)

Though other patterns of parallelism may be found, these three are most commonly used. Occasionally, brief passages or little "essays" add interest and variety; examples of these may be found in the speech attributed to Wisdom in chapter one (verses 20-33), in the lively descriptions of "three things" and "four things" found in chapter thirty, and fairly long passages describing the wiles of the harlot (chapter seven) and the well-loved tribute to a worthy wife found in chapter thirty-one.

Fortunately, the Hebrew form of poetry, the parallelism noted above, can be expressed equally well in other languages. Thus the English translation keeps the form intact and also preserves the concreteness and pictorial quality of the original. Unlike the typical poetry of Western nations, the Jewish poetry preferred specific statements rather than abstractions. The following example illustrates this quality:

Keep my commandments and live;
And my law as the apple of thine eye.
Bind them upon thy fingers;
Write them upon the tablet of thy heart.
Say unto wisdom, Thou art my sister;
And call understanding thy kinswoman.

(7:2-3)

This type of writing is graphic and precise. Its apt use of figures makes the thought memorable.

Another characteristic of the sayings which make up the book of Proverbs is their didacticism. The overriding purpose of the book and the individual passages is to teach what is right and pleasing to God, to encourage the love of wisdom or true understanding, to warn against the sins of pride and the evils of carnality, and to contrast holiness and wickedness, wisdom and folly.

The proverbs are highly moralistic and hortatory. Their method is often a gentle pleading:

My son, keep my words,
And lay up my commandments with thee.

(7:1)

9

Sometimes, however, the method is sharp and direct:

> It is better to dwell in the corner of the housetop,
> Than with a contentious woman in a wide house.
>
> (21:9)

At other times a plain statement of fact is offered for the reader's acceptance:

> It is an honor for a man to keep aloof from strife;
> But every fool will be quarreling.
>
> (20:3)

Whatever type of appeal is chosen, the aim of the several writers remains the same—to influence human thoughts, ideals, and conduct. "This you should do," the writers say; *"that* you should avoid, or suffer the consequences."

The Theme of the Proverbs

If the book of Proverbs can be said to have a theme, certainly the overall theme is wisdom. Over and over in diverse ways, prudential wisdom is extolled—a wisdom that touches every facet of life and brings joy and peace to its possessor. The opening passage in the book declares its aim to be wisdom and good counsel:

> The proverbs of Solomon the son of David, king of Israel:
> To know wisdom and instruction;
> To discern the words of understanding;
> To receive instruction in wise dealing,
> In righteousness and justice and equity;
> To give prudence to the simple,
> To the young man knowledge and discretion:
> That the wise man may hear, and increase in learning;
> And that the man of understanding may attain unto sound
>   counsels:
> To understand a proverb, and a figure,
> The words of the wise, and their dark sayings.
>
> (1:1-6)

This introduction reveals not only the writer's purposes but also one of the methods of instruction, the use of such synonymns as *wisdom, understanding, instruction, knowledge,* and *learning.* Indirectly, the opening also reveals the writer's conception of a proverb as "a figure," "words of the wise," "dark" or symbolic sayings.

The Beginning of Knowledge

Immediately following the opening words of the Proverbs is the familiar statement:

> The fear of Jehovah is the beginning of knowledge;
> But the foolish despise wisdom and instruction.
>
> (1:7)

Modern men often object to the expression "fear God." To those who think of fear only as a negative or destructive force, the idea of fearing God is repellent. They cannot equate fear with love; instead, they consider fear and love to be poles apart. Yet fear of God is consistently taught throughout the Word of God.

Christ expressed quite clearly the meaning of fear or respect for God when he said, "For I am come down from heaven, not to do mine own will, but the will of him that sent me" (John 6:38). In another passage Christ shows that "fear" means to honor: "he [God] hath given all judgment unto the Son that all may honor the Son, even as they honor the Father" (John 5:22, 23). Again, Jesus indicated that his whole purpose in coming to the earth was to do God's will, "for I do always the things that are pleasing to him" (John 8:29).

The quality of awe or high respect is preserved in the old expression "a God-fearing man." To fear God is not to cringe or cower before him as before a tyrant but to hold him in highest esteem, to seek to please him, to obey him because one respects him as a loving Father. The Old Testament story of King Saul, who disobeyed God and stubbornly chose to do his own will rather than keep God's command, illustrates quite well the lack of "fear of God" (see 1 Sam. 15). Thus a deep reverential fear of God was the true foundation of a life of obedience and happiness.

What Wisdom Offers

Three extended passages glorify wisdom. The first is found in Proverbs 1:7-33, where wisdom is personified as a woman who freely offers rich gifts to all who will accept them but who is spurned by fools and scoffers. When men refuse her offerings she declares,

> I also will laugh in the day of your calamity;
> I will mock when your fear cometh.
>
> (1:26)

In their distress men will seek but not find her, for in rejecting wisdom they have rejected the counsels of God and must "eat the fruit

of their own way" and be destroyed by "the careless ease of fools."
So Proverbs opens with an invitation to wisdom. At the same time
it sounds a solemn warning to all who "despise all her reproof."

Chapter three contains a beautiful and most expressive poem on
the blessings to be enjoyed by those who love and cherish wisdom.

> Happy is the man that findeth wisdom,
> And the man that getteth understanding.
> (3:13)

After this impressive beatitude on wisdom, we are reminded of
the gifts which wisdom confers on her lovers. First, wisdom is said
to be superior to silver and fine gold, and "she is more precious than
rubies." Then, nothing man can want is worthy to be compared to
wisdom. Fame, success, and material blessings are fleeting and
cheap in comparison to the abiding riches of wisdom.

> Length of days is in her right hand;
> In her left hand are riches and honor.
> Her ways are ways of pleasantness,
> And all her paths are peace.
> (3:16, 17)

These are truly "the good things of life," the blessings which all
men are seeking—long life, abundance, honor, pleasant ways, and
peace.

The poet then employs a number of figures to give a more fitting
tribute to wisdom: She is called "a tree of life," God's agent in the
creation, and man's most dependable guide (3:18-23).

Moreover, she brings calmness and security:

> Then shalt thou walk in thy way securely,
> And thy foot shall not stumble,
> When thou liest down, thou shalt not be afraid:
> Yea, thou shalt lie down, and thy sleep shall be sweet.
> Be not afraid of sudden fear,
> Neither of the desolation of the wicked, when it cometh:
> For Jehovah will be thy confidence,
> And will keep thy foot from being taken.
> (3:23-26)

This fairly long passage, which occurs in the middle of chapter
three, is justly famous for its rich language and its poetic figures.
The beauty of the language is of course intended to enhance the
loveliness and desirability of wisdom.

It is worth noting, I think, that the "fear of Jehovah" has brought
perfect peace and confidence and driven out the dread of darkness

and "sudden fear." The man who is at peace with God enjoys peace with his own nature and with his neighbors.

The wisdom which is honored throughout the book of Proverbs is a prudential and practical wisdom. It is equated with such terms as understanding, knowledge, instruction, truth, good counsel, discretion, righteousness, and the fear of Jehovah. Thus the ethical and moral sense of the term is emphasized far more than the intellectual or rational idea of wisdom. To the Hebrews it meant a life directed by God's unchanging will and in harmony with his own character. For this reason the writer of Proverbs could say truly,

> The fear of Jehovah is the beginning of wisdom;
> And the knowledge of the Holy One is understanding.
> (9:10)

God is the source of all true wisdom, and God is also the object. Thus to know the statutes or laws of God, and to bring one's life into harmony with his will, was considered not only perfect wisdom but the whole duty of man. Religion, knowledge, right conduct—all these and more were summed up in the general term wisdom and, therefore, bore upon all the day-to-day problems and relationships of men.

Questions

1. To what type of literature does the book of Proverbs belong?
2. Why do you think this book is not studied as much as, say, books of history or prophecy?
3. What patterns in verse arrangement are discernible?
4. Name some significant characteristics of Hebrew poetry.
5. Do you find any evidence of a theme in the Proverbs?
6. Why is the "fear" (respect) of God called the beginning of wisdom?
7. Name some of the rich gifts offered by wisdom.
8. What are the ethical standards of true wisdom?
9. What is the penalty for rejecting wisdom?
10. Does wisdom offer a practical guide for daily living?
11. What is the difference between wisdom and knowledge?

Chapter Two

THE MARKS OF A FRIEND

"A friend loveth at all times. . . ." Proverbs 17:17

THE ESSAYS ON friendship by Bacon, Montaigne, Emerson and others are filled with appealing thoughts and sentiments, but these gentlemen were certainly not the first to survey this field and explore its treasures. In the Old Testament the love of Jonathan and David was so deep and enduring that it became proverbial. The writer of 1 Samuel states that "the soul of Jonathan was knit with the soul of David, and Jonathan loved him as his own soul" (1 Sam. 18:1).

In the Proverbs are found a number of statements about the making and losing of friends. Some of these are notable for their brevity and truthfulness. Some are warnings such as a wise father or mother might give to a son or daughter. How natural and appropriate is the advice: "Thine own friend, and thy father's friend forsake not" (27:10). This is loyalty or faithfulness, the very essence of friendship. Is not the wise man saying, "In the midst of prosperity and among many new admirers, remember the friends of your youth and the friends of the family"? Is not this a clear warning against shallowness and forgetfulness, against self-interest and ingratitude?

Constancy

One quality of true friendship is its constancy. Shakespeare reminds us, "That is not love that alters when it alteration finds." The ancient equivalent of this sentiment is beautifully stated in the Proverbs, "A friend loveth at all times" (17:17). Since human contacts are often used for one's own advantage, our language recognizes the fact by such phrases as "fair-weather friends," or "business friends."

The second half the apothegm "a friend loveth at all times" is the statement, "and a brother is born for adversity." That is, men turn in time of trouble to a friend or brother, expecting solace or help. It is a common mark of our humanity that we want to share good news or misfortune with a friend. Every normal person, whether he's a private in the army or a commander, seeks approbation or consolation from a small circle of friends. One's friends make a victory or achievement sweeter by acclaiming it, and they reduce the pain of disappointment or defeat by sharing it. In our friends we find our favorable characteristics approved and our confidence strengthened; in their kindness we find our weak and less noble qualities minimized and softened. Thus in moments of exultation or in time of need we turn to our friends—and are not disappointed.

Keeping Friends

When one asks, "Why is it that some persons have so many friends and others so few?" perhaps the answer is found in this ringing statement in the Proverbs: "That which maketh a man to be desired is his kindness" (19:22). This is a disposition to deal gently with the faults and infirmities of others. It is gentleness in word and deed. The clever person, the cynic, can find many occasions to ridicule the speech, the mannerisms and the ideas of those around him, and wit is a kind of barbed weapon that strikes at any exposed spot. The sharp-eyed critic can find many "boobs" (one of Mencken's favorite words), but a gracious or kindly person, knowing the hurt that words can inflict, is slow to judge and is kind—even in criticizing. The true gentleman will never, as Newman has said, inflict pain needlessly. To be kind is to be generous, helpful, and, if need be, forgiving.

Candor

Another aspect of friendship is frankness, not hiding the truth when it ought to be told. Experience proves the wisdom of the saying, "Faithful are the wounds of a friend, but the kisses of an enemy are profuse" (27:6). Men go to a doctor to learn the truth about matters affecting the body or the health and to a minister or spiritual counselor to get helpful advice on spiritual problems.

Happy is the person who has a friend to whom he can go for frank, objective counsel, even though this may concern some wrong one has done and the words of the friend may be hard to accept. It is far better to be rebuked, to be told plainly that one's attitude or behavior is wrong, than to go on in a course leading to graver wrong or disaster. One can trust his friend because the friend has only one principle of conduct—to seek what is best for his confidant. Thus his criticisms or reproofs are "faithful." We value the counsels of those who try to be quite fair and objective with us, even though the appraisal may temporarily bring pain and mortification.

Closely related to this ability to accept criticism or correction is the humbling of oneself to admit error or sin.

> He that covereth his transgressions shall not prosper;
> But whoso confesseth and forsaketh them shall obtain mercy.
> (28:13)

In many passages in the Proverbs the wise man is distinguished from the fool in that the former "tries" his words, avoids rashness and lies, and is ready at all times to admit error and learn from those who offer good counsel. "Where no wise guidance is, the people falleth; but in the multitude of counsellors there is safety" (11:14).

As noted earlier, the method of instruction used in a major part of the Proverbs is that of a father addressing his son. Again and again, such expressions as "My son, keep my words" and "Now therefore, my sons, hearken unto me" indicate that age and experience are speaking to youth and inexperience. Hundreds of statements are frankly hortatory; they are direct, personal, and explicit. Some advice of this kind is given regarding friendship.

> Make no friendship with a man that is given to anger;
> And with a wrathful man thou shalt not go:
> Lest thou learn his ways,
> And get a snare to thy soul.
> (22:24, 25)

Again the writer advises:

> He that goeth about as a talebearer revealeth secrets;
> Therefore company not with him that openeth wide his lips.
> (20:19)

> A perverse man scattereth abroad strife;
> And a whisperer separateth chief friends.
> (16:28)

The Marks of a Friend

Friends are therefore to be chosen because they are upright, honest, God-fearing, and worthy of one's highest trust. The selfish, carnal, undisciplined man is to be avoided, for he is the "fool" so often described and warned against in the Proverbs.

Questions

1. What is notable about the friendship of Jonathan and David?
2. What do you consider to be the first requirement of friendship?
3. Name other important characteristics of friendship.
4. Comment on the place of kindness in human relations.
5. Can real friendship stand the test of frankness? Why or why not?
6. What qualities do you ask—and offer—in friendship?
7. What types of friends must a wise man avoid?
8. Who is the "friend that sticketh closer than a brother"?

Chapter Three

THE INNER MAN

The spirit of man is the lamp of Jehovah
Searching all his innermost parts.
Proverbs 20:27

MUCH IS SAID about the "heart" in the Proverbs, even as in the Psalms and many of the prophetic books. The heart is said to think, to believe, to trust, to love and hate, to envy, to plan and act, to become hard or bitter. As one considers the various abilities attributed to the heart, it becomes evident that by this term the ancient writers meant the mind or reason as well as the emotions and will.

Psychologically, the heart seems to be identified in scripture with intelligence (reasoning, reflecting, understanding), the emotions (loving, fearing, hating), and the will (accepting or rejecting what is offered, planning, and carrying out one's decisions). In truth, the heart, so understood, is the essential or inner man, the real person —as distinguished from the visible man. The term heart, therefore, referred to what we today call personality. The attitudes of the heart made individuals kind or hateful, cheerful or morose, righteous or wicked.

The crucial importance of the inner mind or spirit is indicated in the injunction "Keep thy heart with all diligence" (variant reading: "Above all thou guardest"), "for out of it are the issues of life." Thus the heart is declared to be the fountain of life or the source of all conduct. With the heart man loves or rejects God, with the heart he plans evil or shows mercy, and by cultivating the good intentions of the heart man becomes a noble person; just as by hardening his heart, as Pharaoh did, he brings wrath and destruction

18

upon himself. The motives of pride, arrogance, justice, love and pity, hatred and rebellion all issue from the good or evil heart. This being true, no other task in life is so important as keeping the heart clean, humble, just, and benevolent.

Since this is a timeless truth, it agrees perfectly with our Lord's teaching concerning the hidden springs of conduct:

> For out of the heart come forth evil thoughts, murders,
> adulteries, fornications, thefts, false witness, railings:
> these are the things which defile the man. . . .
>
> (Matt. 15:19, 20)

Again Christ said, in quoting from Isaiah, "This people honoreth me with their lips, but their hearts are far from me" (Matt. 13:8). One of the objects of God's hatred, so we are told in Proverbs, is "a heart that deviseth wicked purposes" (6:18).

Two Kinds of Hearts

Christ viewed men as having either "good and honest" hearts or "evil" hearts. He drew an analogy from nature: "a good tree cannot bring forth evil fruit, neither can a corrupt tree bring forth good fruit" (Matt. 7:18). And He added a law by which men might judge the goodness or badness of the human heart when He said, "By their fruits ye shall know them."

In the same way the writer of Proverbs calls upon man to accept God's counsel and enjoy his favor:

> Trust in Jehovah with all thy heart,
> And lean not upon thine own understanding:
> In all thy ways acknowledge him,
> And he will direct thy paths.   (3:5, 6)

Again, the thought which may properly be called the theme of Proverbs, advises men:

> The fear of Jehovah is the beginning of knowledge,
> But the foolish despise wisdom and instruction.
>
> (1:7)

In pleading with man to seek God's will and to "search for her as for hid treasure," Solomon declares:

> For Jehovah giveth wisdom;
> Out of his mouth cometh knowledge and understanding;
> He layeth up sound wisdom for the upright;
> He is a shield to them that walk in integrity.
>
> (2:6, 7)

In the first third of the book of Proverbs countless blessings are promised to those who love God's will and keep it. They are promised peace, loving favor, length of days, an honorable name, great abundance, and glory. But if blessings and honor are the reward of the righteous, the wicked have only contempt and cursing:

> For the perverse is an abomination to Jehovah;
> But his friendship is with the upright.
> The curse of Jehovah is in the house of the wicked . . .
> Surely he scoffeth at the scoffers;
> But he giveth grace unto the lowly.
>
> (3:32-34)

It is not surprising to find that it is man's heart, not his reputation, which God judges.

> Sheol and Abaddon are before Jehovah,
> How much more then the hearts of the children of men!
>
> (15:11)

And further on,

> The refining pot is for silver, and the furnace for gold;
> But Jehovah trieth the hearts.
>
> (17:3)

The idea of judgment is often presented in this book. Sometimes it is the temporal judgment of men, who mete out rewards and punishments according to human merit, but far more impressive are the passages setting forth the judgment of God on evildoers, as for example:

> He that being often reproved hardeneth his neck
> Shall suddenly be destroyed, and that without remedy.
>
> (29:1)

Man's Self-knowledge

From another point of view, the Proverbs reveal many interesting insights about man's spirit. Each of these statements is worthy of more than passing notice. Here, for example, are some that touch on "heaviness of heart":

> Heaviness in the heart of a man maketh it stoop;
> But a good word maketh it glad.
>
> (12:25)

> Hope deferred maketh the heart sick;
> But when the desire cometh, it is a tree of life.
>
> (13:12)

Even in laughter the heart is sorrowful;
And the end of mirth is heaviness.

(14:13)

It is common knowledge that a burdened heart will show itself in one's attitudes and behavior. The heaviness spoken of in Proverbs 12:25 may come from sorrow, from care, from guilt, a sense of rejection or failure, or from many personal problems. The result ("make it stoop") is what we call mental depression. When cares press heavily or one feels that he has done some wrong or brought shame upon himself, the natural result is discouragement or heaviness of heart. One cause cited for this dispiritedness is frustration — "hope deferred," which makes the heart sick. An expected reward fails to come, the ministrations of the doctor fail to bring health, or some promise that once made life bright has not been fulfilled — such experiences are the common lot of mankind.

Yet the picture has another side. In the first passage noted above, "a good word" gladdens the heavy heart. How remarkable that a single word can often dispel the gloomy thoughts and bring a song to the heart. This may be a word of praise, of confidence expressed by a friend, or a promise of something to come. Many years ago I was impressed by the remark of an uneducated fisherman in Alaska about the response of a child to a small gift. "It takes so little to make them glad," he said, "and so little to disappoint them." We who are much older and wiser in the world's ways are not substantially different. Often a simple but sincere compliment can brighten one's day, and may even be remembered for years.

The observation that "even in laughter the heart is sorrowful" can be illustrated in the biographies of many who have won acclaim as humorists but laughed only to hide their sorrow. One of the most notable examples of the truth is seen in the life and writing of Mark Twain, who became world famous for his droll speeches and comic portrayal of many types of humanity. But beneath the wit, the tall tale, or the caricature of society which thousands admired was a deeply passionate spirit which was often saddened or revolted by man's injustice, greed, contempt for "lower classes," and lack of humanity. His letters and autobiography reveal a man keenly sensitive to the meanness and depravity of man, though at the same time he hid his darker musings behind a flow of stories and speeches on the lecture platform that brought mirth to millions and fame to himself.

If "hope deferred" brings heartache, then on the other hand fulfillment brings peace and joy:

The desire accomplished is sweet to the soul . . . (13:19).

This basic truth of man's nature is stated so simply as to seem obvious. Nevertheless, it is an insight of great value, and modern writers—both in theology and psychology—have said the same thing, though in more erudite fashion. Tillich said, "Where there is joy there is fulfillment, and where there is fulfillment there is joy." One requirement of any good job is that it give the worker a sense of accomplishment—something to show for his labor. When one's task is so small or limited that he cannot see the end result of his labor, the task becomes burdensome and perhaps intolerable. As a boy I used to find that plowing gave me a deep satisfaction, for at the end of the day I (and my dad) could see just how much I had done.

One of the reasons why graduation—at whatever level—is observed with pomp and ceremony is that it represents for all the graduates the attainment of a worthwhile goal. They have shown purpose and discipline through several years of activity (often quite demanding work), and the public exercises are planned to give them a sense of achievement and honor.

The Cheerful Heart

The passages dealing with the downcast heart are more than balanced by those which comment on the buoyant or happy heart. Let us take two:

A glad heart maketh a cheerful countenance;
But by sorrow of heart the spirit is broken.
(15:13)

A cheerful heart is a good medicine;
But a broken spirit drieth up the bones.
(17:22)

Once again the message is expressed in contrasts. The glad or grateful heart expresses itself in the countenance; the joy is reflected in the eyes and the smile. Sorrow and shame are likewise registered in the face, so that many of our common expressions are based on what we read in the faces of those about us. We ask, for example, "What is he so happy about?" or "What do you think has gone wrong with him?"

Who knows how many sermons—or lessons on mental health—have been based on the text that "a cheerful (or merry) heart is a good medicine"? This statement applies first to the one who has a cheerful heart; he is blessed physically and emotionally by having a happy outlook. He will enjoy life far more than his doleful neighbor, and in addition he will probably live much longer. But the benefits of the cheerful disposition do not end with the possessor. His happy smile or cheery ways will brighten the lives of all those who come in contact with him. We are attracted by the gay or spirited attitude of the person who finds something good to say, no matter what the problem may be, for we instinctively like laughter better than sorrow or sarcasm.

Many times strong, healthy persons, who through thoughtlessness complain about small problems or discomforts, are shamed by the cheerfulness and good humor of an invalid or someone with serious physical handicaps. Years ago I knew a girl whose body was so twisted that she could not walk and her fingers so deformed that she could not do most things that other children do. Although sadly deformed and a shut-in, she had a keen mind, completed grade school and high school under the tutelage of teachers who came to her home, and at fifteen published a delightful book of verses composed between her fifth and fourteenth year. Though she used a typewriter by punching the keys with the eraser end of a pencil grasped awkwardly in her right hand, she rose triumphantly above her handicap and made her life worthwhile. Her cheerfulness was never-failing, and when she met friends or strangers, as she often did when her mother took her out in her wheelchair, she impressed them by her gaiety and pleasant disposition. Her little volume of poems is a testament to her courage and her joyful outlook on life. There is not one word of self-pity or complaint in the book, and the reader might not ever know of her handicaps except for the foreword written by a friend.

> All the days of the afflicted are evil;
> But he that is of a cheerful heart hath a continual feast.
> (15:15)

This verse suggests that the depressed or gloomy live in an atmosphere of darkness and evil, while the cheerful person enjoys a "continual feast." One eats the bread of discontent; the other enjoys the best things of life. The dividends of happiness are reserved for those who maintain, even in difficult times, a serene and happy spirit. Even though the same troubles may fall upon two people in similar circumstances, one may become hardened, bitter, and broken, while the other responds bravely and successfully to the disappointments and heartaches that destroy many men. When the circumstances are identical, the difference lies only in the heart. How heartening is the life of a Helen Keller or a blind Milton!

Questions

1. Explain the importance of "the heart" as this term is used in the Bible.
2. Does the term "heart" seem to be the equivalent of what is today called "personality"? Give reasons for your answer.
3. What kind of heart is pleasing to God?
4. How can one "keep" his heart? Why is this supremely important?
5. What is meant by hardening the heart? Give examples.
6. Explain such terms as "heavy-hearted," "sick at heart," and "half-hearted."
7. What are some ways to gladden the heart — your own or another's?
8. Discuss the value of a "cheerful heart"—in the individual life, the home, the church.
9. Cite examples you know personally of a "change of heart."
10. How may one enjoy a "continual feast"?

Chapter Four

GLIMPSES OF GOD

The horse is prepared against the day of battle;
But victory is of Jehovah.   Proverbs 21:31

ALTHOUGH THE Proverbs were written to glorify wisdom and to warn men against wrongdoing, the nature of God is often alluded to. Though earth, not heaven, is the apparent setting of this book, God's ways and works are frequently mentioned. The Creator and Judge of mankind stands, one may say, in the background, approving or disapproving and meting out to men their just deserts. Happy is the man who early learns to "fear" Jehovah and to keep his laws. Such a man shall be blessed in all his doings.

The revelation of God in these pages is incidental but clear, and is consistent with the view of God presented in the law and the prophets. He is shown to be powerful, all-seeing, just or righteous, hating evil, but merciful to those who love truth and justice. He is the source of all true wisdom, the creator of all men, and the protector of the upright.

The God of the Hebrew fathers was not limited in knowledge or power. The incontinent man is warned that "the ways of man are before the eyes of Jehovah" (5:21) and man must answer for his sin. The immediacy of God, from whom nothing is hid, is graphically stated in these words:

The eyes of Jehovah are in every place,
Keeping watch upon the evil and the good.
(15:3)

Even the underworld, the place of departed spirits, is said to be watched by God:

> Sheol and Abaddon are before Jehovah;
> How much more then the hearts of the children of men..
>
> (15:11)

The faith expressed in these passages, that man's thoughts as well as his deeds are all known to God, serves as a strong motive to righteous living. If, as David has observed,

> But the darkness hideth not from thee,
>   But the night shineth as the day:
> The darkness and the light are both alike
>   to thee.   (Psalm 139:12)

then man has every reason to control his animal nature and to live as a creature of God. This concept, which of course agrees with the Christian view of life, is higher and stronger than any human law in directing and controlling the believer's life. As one of the English divines has said, "The fear of God is the only thing that can keep one honest in the dark." Since God "searchest out my path and my lying down and knoweth all my ways," and it is impossible to flee from him or escape his sight, I am kept from many of the follies and sins of godless men.

God is Strong

Men are warned against "robbing the poor" and "entering the fields of the fatherless," because "their Redeemer is strong" (23:11) and will take the side of the oppressed. In many passages God is shown to be concerned about wrongs committed against the poor and defenseless.

> The way of Jehovah is a stronghold to the upright;
> But it is destruction to the workers of iniquity.
>
> (10:29)

He will show himself strong to those who put their trust in him. A passage of rare beauty offers comfort to the faithful.

> Be not afraid of sudden fear,
> Neither of the desolation of the
>   wicked when it cometh;
> For Jehovah will be thy confidence,
> And will keep thy foot from being taken.
>
> (3:25, 26)

One of the most striking expressions of God's power is put in epigrammatic fashion:

> The horse is prepared against the day of battle:
> But victory [or deliverance] is of Jehovah.
>
> (21:31)

He is Just

God's justice is as notable as his strength. Abraham's conception of God's fair dealing with man was put in a searching question: "shall not the Judge of all the earth do right?" (Gen. 18:25). The messages of the prophets, of David in the Psalms and of the writers in Proverbs all agree that God will reward the faithful and punish the wrongdoers. One of the clearest statements of this principle in Proverbs affirms the equity of God's judgment:

> If thou sayest, Behold we knew not this;
> Doth not he that weigheth the hearts consider it? . . .
> And shall he not render to every man according to his work?
>
> (24:12)

Some sins will be punished in the day of judgment, but others bear fruit in this life. Consider the following statements:

> A man shall be satisfied with good by the fruit of his mouth;
> And the doings of a man's hands shall be rendered unto him.
>
> (12:14)

> Good understanding giveth favor;
> But the way of the transgressor is hard.
>
> (13:15)

Thus kindness and generosity were said to bring rewards to men in this life, and such sins as gluttony, drunkenness, and sloth would bring shame, physical suffering, and penury upon the evildoers. For example, the wise man was promised riches, long life, and honor; but the fool (who is characterized by perversity and unconcern for all that is good) is promised beatings, sorrow, and destruction. The good man enjoys the fruit of a righteous life, but the wicked find only bitterness and affliction.

> The curse of Jehovah is in the house of the wicked;
> But he blesseth the habitation of the righteous.
>
> (3:33)

> They would none of my counsel,
> They despised all my reproof.
> Therefore they shall eat of the fruit of their way,
> And be filled with their own devices.
>
> (1:30, 31)

An excellent summary of God's justice is found in chapter two of Proverbs:

> He layeth up sound wisdom for the upright;
> He is a shield to them that walk in integrity;
> That he may guard the paths of justice,
> And preserve the way of his saints.
> Then shalt thou understand righteousness and justice,
> And equity, yea, every good path.
>
> (2:7-9)

If a man can be judged by what he loves, God can be judged by what he hates.

What God Hates

In the Proverbs many specific sins are singled out as hateful to God (perverse lips, unjust balance, a haughty attitude, to cite a few examples.) In one of the several "clusters" found in the Proverbs seven acts hateful to God are listed:

> There are six things which Jehovah hateth;
> Yea, seven which are an abomination unto him:
> Haughty eyes, a lying tongue,
> And hands that shed innocent blood;
> A heart that deviseth wicked purposes,
> Feet that are swift in running to mischief,
> A false witness that uttereth lies,
> And he that soweth discord among brethren.
>
> (6:16-19)

Obviously, this list does not attempt to name all that is offensive to God. Instead, it singles out certain attitudes as well as actions productive of evil: haughtiness or pride, lying, murder, a reprobate heart, a love of mischief or wrongdoing, and the sowing of discord among peaceable people. The summary given here contains six rather than seven offenses because the original list refers twice to lying—in lines three and seven above. It is noticeable that several of the more common sins, such as adultery, gluttony, stealing, and oppression of the poor are not mentioned here. The wrongs that are specified are primarily those of evil attitudes: arrogance, injustice, a wicked heart, and breaching the peace.

Among the other things described as abominations to God are evil men (3:32), perverse hearts (11:20), the sacrifice of the wicked (15:8), false balances (11:1) and false weights (20:10, 23) used to defraud the unwary, and lying lips (12:22). Here are two categories of evil: attitudes offensive to God, including even the sacrifices made by wicked man, and sins against persons.

His Mercy

Another attribute of God is mercy, for which humility is the most common prerequisite.

> All the ways of a man are clean in his own eyes;
> But Jehovah weigheth the spirits.
> Commit thy works unto Jehovah,
> And thy purposes shall be established.
> (16:2, 3)

> By mercy and truth iniquity is atoned for;
> And by the fear of Jehovah men depart from evil.
> (16:6)

The joining of mercy, (God's part) and truth (man's part) in the act of atonement is comparable to Paul's declaration that men are saved through grace (God's gift) and faith (man's response) (see Eph. 2:8). From another point of view, mercy is not automatic; man must humble himself or seek God's forgiveness in order to receive it.

> Jehovah is far from the wicked,
> But he heareth the prayer of the righteous.
> (15:29)

> He that covereth his transgressions shall not prosper;
> But whoso confesseth and forsaketh them shall obtain mercy.
> (28:13)

In Proverbs God is called the creator of *all* men:

> The rich and the poor meet together:
> Jehovah is the maker of them all.
> (22:2)

> The poor man and the oppressor meet together;
> Jehovah lighteneth the eyes of them both.
> (29:13)

> He that oppresseth the poor reproacheth his maker.
> (14:31)

Human distinctions of class and color are of no consequence in the sight of God, who looks not on man's appearance but on the heart (1 Sam. 16:7). The poor and the rich, the slave and free man, the

29

black and white are all acceptable to God when they obey his teachings and show respect for other men. In the words of Malachi,

> Have we not all one father? hath not one God
> created us? why do we deal treacherously every
> man against his brother profaning the covenant
> of our fathers?   (Malachi 2:10)

Again, the teaching of the Proverbs is seen to agree with the highest ideals of the prophets.

God is a shield to the just man, a strong tower to those who seek refuge in him. As noted earlier, God offers protection to the faithful but turns his face against the evildoer. This theme may be traced through the warp and woof of the Proverbs.

Respect for God

Respect for God, or reverence, is often expressed in this book as "the fear of Jehovah." This is not a cringing or craven fear but a wholesome attitude of trust and confidence. It can be described as taking God at his word. For this reason the "fear of the Lord" is always extolled as proper, wise, and rewarding:

> The fear of Jehovah is the beginning of knowledge.
>   (1:7)
> The fear of Jehovah is the beginning of wisdom;
> And knowledge of the Holy one is understanding.
>   (9:10)

> Fear Jehovah and depart from evil:
> It will be health to thy navel,
> And marrow to thy bones.
>   (3:7, 8)

This kind of holy fear is described as a "fountain of life" (14:27). It also brings, in the language of the writer, "health to thy navel and marrow to thy bones." This may be understood as meaning that man's life will be blessed if he keeps the laws of God.

> The fear of Jehovah prolongeth days;
> But the years of the wicked shall be shortened.
>   (10:27)

True Wisdom

One of the interesting observations growing out of this study of the Proverbs is that in a great many instances wisdom is personified and seems to be identical with God. In chapter one, for instance,

Wisdom cries in the streets and asks why men have rejected knowledge and reproof. Then, it warns that such rejection will be inevitably punished:

> But ye set at nought all my counsel,
> And would none of my reproof:
> I also will laugh in the day of your calamity;
> I will mock when your fear cometh;
> For that they hated knowledge,
> And did not choose the fear of Jehovah.
>   (1:26, 25, 29)

Note that Wisdom is the speaker here (verses 20, 24), but in verse 29 the rejecting of wisdom is the rejection of Jehovah. The remainder of the passage reinforces the idea that the punishment for refusing wise counsel is the same as rejecting God's way. Chapters two and three continue to use the terms "my words" and "my law" as the equivalent of God's revelation, even though there has been no change in the speaker. The opening of chapter two pleads for the acceptance of wisdom and discernment, and then adds:

> Then shalt thou understand the fear of Jehovah,
> And find the knowledge of God.
> For Jehovah giveth wisdom;
> Out of his mouth cometh knowledge and understanding.
>   (2:5, 6)

The rewards of wisdom detailed in chapter three are the same as those elsewhere promised to the obedient: health, long life, honors, peace, and security.

Personification in Hebrew poetry is a popular device. In the Psalms the earth, the trees, the waters are called upon to praise God (see Psalm 98, and Isaiah 55:12 for notable passages of this kind). In the same way Wisdom is personified in the first three chapters of Proverbs, reaching a climax in chapter three. Here "she is more precious than rubies"; in one hand she holds "length of days" and in the other "riches and honor." Moreover, her ways lead to "pleasantness," "and all her paths are peace." Thus to possess Wisdom is to enjoy the best gifts of life, and she is declared to be a "tree of life to them that lay hold upon her" (3:18).

Finally, the relation of Wisdom to God is set out in verse 19: "Jehovah by wisdom founded the earth . . . and established the heavens." Wisdom thus seems to be a servant of God in the creation

31

—a kind of assistant in the original works of God. This thought is further advanced in chapter eight, as follows:

> Jehovah possessed me in the beginning of his way,
> Before his works of old.
> I was set up from everlasting, from the beginning,
> Before the earth was.
>
> (8:22, 23)
>
> When he established the heavens, I was there:
> When he set a circle upon the face of the deep . . .
> When he marked out the foundations of the earth;
> Then was I by him, as a master workman;
> And I was daily his delight,
> Rejoicing always before him,
> Rejoicing in his habitable earth;
> And my delight was with the sons of men.
>
> (8:27, 29c-31)

There is but a step from this position to the New Testament teaching that Christ was with the Father in the creation, "through whom also he made the worlds" (Heb. 1:2). John's gospel asserts that Christ, the Logos, was with God in the beginning, and "all things were made through him; and without him was not anything made that hath been made" (John 1:3). Paul further declares in 1 Corinthians 1:24 that "unto them that are called, both Jews and Greeks, Christ [is] the power of God and the wisdom of God." Again he says, in verse 30, "But of him are ye in Christ Jesus, who was made *unto us wisdom from God,* and righteousness and sanctification, and redemption. . . ."

Christians see in the person and work of Christ, the "wisdom and power" of God and the means of man's redemption. The Logos of John is identical with the wisdom described by Paul as God's way of calling and sanctifying men. The heavenly wisdom, Christ's gospel, stands in sharp contrast to the earthly, sensual wisdom of the Greeks. Man's wisdom is not only foolish and weak, but futile. The wisdom from above—incarnate in Christ—is the reconciling and redeeming power which Christ exerts in the lives of those who accept him. In essence, therefore, Christ is prefigured in such passages in Proverbs as:

> Blessed is the man that heareth me . . .
> For whoso findeth me findeth life,
> And shall obtain favor of Jehovah.
> But he that sinneth against me wrongeth his own soul:
> All they that hate me love death.
>
> (8:34a,35,36)

He is the source of life, peace, and joy. He is, in truth, the full expression of "the wisdom that is from above."

Questions

1. What characteristics of God are revealed in the Proverbs?
2. Where can men hide from God? Read Psalms 139.
3. What arguments are advanced to keep man from sinning against his neighbor?
4. Discuss God's justice. Is it always apparent?
5. Does judgment wait for the final reckoning at the end of time? Cite examples for your statements.
6. Name some acts and attitudes hateful to God.
7. Can you distinguish several categories of sin?
8. On what conditions may man expect mercy?
9. How does God view class consciousness or respect of persons? Consider, besides Proverbs, James 2:1-4.
10. Discuss the heavenly wisdom, i.e., that which comes from above, as prefiguring Christ.

Chapter Five

A MAN AND HIS MONEY

There is that scattereth, and increaseth yet more . . .
(Proverbs 11:24)

SINCE THE PURPOSE of the Proverbs was to show men the way to conduct their lives, money and property are discussed repeatedly and with relish. Next to wisdom, which is the *summum bonum* of life, a good living, honestly acquired and rightly dispensed, is lauded as one of the highest ideals on earth. Indeed, riches and honor are held by the writer to be signs of God's approval and blessing: "the crown of the wise is their riches" (14:15), and wisdom is said to offer both riches and honor (3:15).

In one of the most personal statements in the book (attributed to Águr) the ideal state is thus described:

Give me neither poverty nor riches;
Feed me with the food that is needful to me:
Lest I be full and deny thee and say, Who is Jehovah?
Or lest I be poor, and steal,
And use profanely the name of my God.
(30:8b, 9)

A middle course between the two economic extremes seemed to this ancient writer to be the best possible life. Too great prosperity would, he feared, make him self-sufficient and indifferent toward God—one of the problems affecting the life of millions of Americans today. On the other hand, poverty might likewise lead to stealing and to denial of God. Who can say whether great riches or grinding poverty is more likely to turn one from God, in the

34

first case because a man "doesn't need God" ("I'm doing very well, thank you!") or conversely because one feels that God has forsaken him and left him to starve?

If the great majority of the Jews felt that prosperity was a sign of God's favor, it was only natural to conclude that poverty (unless merited by one's own sloth or mismanagement) was evidence of wrongdoing or hidden sin. Under such circumstances men would be tempted to gain wealth, if necessary, by dishonest practices and oppression. And poverty, besides being a social stigma, would seem to the majority to be a punishment justly inflicted by God upon evildoers. Perhaps this attitude explains the caution given in these words:

> Weary not thyself to be rich;
> . . . .
> Wilt thou set thine eyes upon that which is not?
> For riches certainly make themselves wings,
> Like an eagle that flieth toward heaven.
> $\qquad$ (23:4, 5)

Again the writer makes clear that the poor are not to be despised, for they too are children of God:

> The rich and poor meet together:
> Jehovah is the maker of them all.
> $\qquad$ (22:2)

And many passages, as we shall see later, call for justice and generosity in the treatment of the poor.

Some Basic Truths

Before turning to a consideration of the misuse of money, it may be profitable to examine some of the explicit teachings about work, providing for one's needs, and caring for property. Every reader of Proverbs will remember the lowly, hard-working ant which is presented as a symbol of the provident man:

> Go to the ant, thou sluggard;
> Consider her ways and be wise;
> Which having no chief, overseer or ruler,
> Provideth her bread in the summer,
> And gathereth her food in the harvest.
> $\qquad$ (6:6-8; see also 30:25)

One attribute of the wise man is that he looks beyond the present moment; he plans his life and his work to accomplish certain purposes.

In all labor there is profit;
But the talk of the lips tendeth only to penury.
(14:23)

There is precious treasure and oil in the dwelling of the wise;
But a foolish man swalloweth it up.
(21:20)

The laggard, the lazy, put off work until the harvest is over, or else work haphazardly:

He becometh poor that worketh with a slack hand;
But the hand of the diligent maketh rich.
He that gathereth in summer is a wise son;
But he that sleepeth in harvest is a son that causeth shame.
(10:4-5)

In vivid language the weed-choked field of the sluggard is described:

I went by the field of the sluggard,
And by the vineyard of the man void of understanding;
And, lo, it was all grown over with thorns,
The face thereof was covered with nettles,
And the stone wall thereof was broken down.

(24:30-31)

This field appeared to the writer to be a parable on the way to lose one's living:

Then I beheld, and considered well;
I saw and received instruction:
Yet a little sleep, a little slumber,
A little folding of the hands to sleep;
So shall thy poverty come as a robber,
And thy want as an armed man.

(24:32-34)

Earning One's Keep

Three virtues having to do with labor and property are extolled in the Proverbs: working to provide for oneself, taking due care to preserve and increase one's property, and using wealth as a steward of God's bounty. All of these are wise and practical teachings that are needed in this generation as much as in ancient Israel.

Having shown the need for honest and diligent labor, we turn now to caring for property.

Whoso keepeth the fig-tree shall eat the fruit thereof.
(27:18)

Be thou diligent to know the state of thy flocks,
And look well to thy herds;
For riches are not for ever;
And doth the crown endure unto all generations?
The hay is carried, and the tender grass showeth itself,
And the herbs of the mountains are gathered in.
The lambs are for thy clothing,
And the goats are the price of the field;
And there will be goats' milk enough for thy food, for the
    food of thy household,
And maintenance for thy maidens.
(27:23-27)
He that tilleth his land shall have plenty of bread;
But he that followeth after vain persons shall have
    poverty enough.   (28:19)

Many lands have such proverbs as "Take care of your sheep
(cattle, herds) and they will take care of you," and "It isn't the
land but the man that makes a good farm." The ideal of careful
husbandry was particularly applicable in a small, nearly arid land
such as Palestine. There the soil, the water, wood, and all products
of the field had to be conserved to sustain man and beast. Nothing
could be wasted, and for this reason squandering was looked upon
as a grievous wrong. The very abundance of some lands, like our
own America, has produced ruinous waste of natural resources. The
early settler generally believed that the forests were limitless, the land
was almost boundless, and the streams would never run dry. Late
in the twentieth century our economists and conservationists are
trying to reverse this long-established view of the superabundance of
natural wealth, and our children and grandchildren may need to
learn again the biblical virtues of thrift and careful husbandry of
all God's gifts—land, water, natural beauty, as well as the products
of the earth.

Warnings to the Would-be Rich

In the Old Testament, wealth and the love of wealth are not condemned as evil. Instead, such wrongs as dishonest dealings, deceit,
lying, usury, and injustice—especially in the treatment of the poor
or defenseless—are scorned.

Better is a little, with righteousness,
Than great revenues with injustice.
(16:8)

A just balance and scales are Jehovah's;
All the weights of the bag are his work.
(16:11)

37

> Diverse weights are an abomination to Jehovah;
> And a false balance is not good.
>
> (20:23)

One kind of dishonesty practiced in ancient days was the removing or shifting of landmarks so as to change the boundaries of property. In a day when it was not possible to fix markers in concrete or to keep records as definitive as those in use today, the destroying or changing of boundary markers was a serious offense. Thus it is not surprising to read such admonitions as these:

> Remove not the ancient landmark which thy fathers have set.
>
> (22:28)

> Remove not the ancient landmark;
> And enter not into the field of the fatherless:
> For their Redeemer is strong;
> He will plead their cause against thee.
>
> (23:10, 11)

In the first quotation a simple prohibition is given, but the second one adds a warning against taking the property of the fatherless and then states that God will champion the rights of the poor or helpless. Thus law among the ancient Jews involved not merely legal but ethical considerations. To the corpus of the law the teachers or rabbis added the conscience of righteous men.

Sundry other proverbs express this same concern for what is morally right:

> Rob not the poor, because he is poor;
> Neither oppress the afflicted in the gate:
> For Jehovah will plead their cause,
> And despoil of life those that despoil them.
>
> (22:22, 23)

> To have respect of persons is not good;
> Neither that a man should transgress for a piece of bread.
> He that hath an evil eye hasteth after riches,
> And knoweth not that want shall come upon him.
>
> (28:21, 22)

> Whoso robbeth his father or his mother, and saith,
>   It is no transgression,
> The same is the companion of a destroyer.
>
> (28:24)

We may be astonished to find that stealing from one's own parents was prohibited by law, yet experience, even in this enlightened age, shows beyond any question that some children will—by legal or illegal means—take the property of those who have given them life.

Even in the time of Christ, the Savior found it necessary to condemn forthrightly the practice of Corban, that is, asserting that one's goods or wealth had been devoted to God (perhaps "promised" is the better word) and therefore the son or daughter felt no responsibility for the care of aged parents (see Mark 7:9-13; note also Proverbs 30:11-14). Christ exposed this subterfuge as a calculated evasion of the fifth commandment: "Honor thy father and thy mother," and he further accused these sophists of putting tradition ahead of God's law.

Remembering the Source of Our Blessings

Although the charge has been made by some students of Proverbs that the book contains little theological teaching, a close study will reveal that the writers had a firm faith in God as just, righteous, omniscient, and omnipotent. These concepts have been dealt with in another chapter. Here it is sufficient to say that in Proverbs the sins against oneself or against others are reprobated not only for prudential reasons (one's reputation will suffer, for example) but for very good theological reasons as well ("To do righteousness and justice is more acceptable to Jehovah than sacrifice," 21:3). Thus a wrong done to a lowly person is the same as though it were done to God, and mercy or benevolence shown to the needy is also considered as though it were done for God.

If we may judge from the prominence given in the Proverbs to the subject of hoarding, it was one of the gravest wrongs among God's people.

> Honor Jehovah with thy substance,
> And with the firstfruits of all thine increase:
> So shall thy barns be filled with plenty,
> And thy vats shall overflow with new wine.
>   (3:9, 10)

The setting of this passage is a plea to hear and to observe God's laws. In the opening verses the son is exhorted to remember God's commandments and the rewards attached to them—

> For length of days, and years of life,
> And peace, will they add to thee.
>   (3:2)

And lest one be tempted to substitute his own will in place of God's law, the writer adds:

> Trust in Jehovah with all thy heart,
> And lean not upon thine own understanding

In all thy ways acknowledge him,
And he will direct thy path.
(3:5-6)

Man's first obligation is to God. The first commandment in the Decalogue as well as the teaching of Christ in answer to what is the great commandment (Matt. 22:35-38) make this clear. One expression of man's love or gratitude is his "giving to God," though, of course, strictly speaking it is not possible to give God anything. "He is not served by men's hands, as though he needed anything." Yet he has always required man to give of his substance or income, as many passages in both the old and new testaments prove. Significantly, these gifts or offerings should come before all other needs and interests. Note that the passage above calls (as the Levitical law did) for the "firstfruits of all thine increase." It is also worth noting that the last book of the Old Testament includes a declaration from God to his people concerning the matter of their robbing God (see Mal. 3:7-12).

Another passage which reproves hoarding and holds out blessings to the faithful and generous person declares

There is that scattereth and increaseth yet more;
And there is that withholdeth more than is meet,
    but it tendeth only to want.
The liberal soul shall be made fat;
And he that watereth shall be watered also himself.
He that withholdeth grain, the people shall curse him;
But blessing shall be upon the head of him that selleth it.

He that trusteth in his riches shall fall;
But the righteous shall flourish as the green leaf.
(11:24-26, 28)

Consider also these proverbial truths on giving or generosity:

There is that coveteth greedily all the day long;
But the righteous giveth and withholdeth not.
(21:26)

He that hath a bountiful eye shall be blessed;
For he giveth of his bread to the poor.
(22:9)

He that hath pity upon the poor lendeth unto Jehovah,
And his good deed will he pay him again.
(19:17)

The language in these quotations is both picturesque and powerful. God promises to bless those who put mercy and compassion above

40

selfish profit; he promises abundance to those who give unstintingly
to the needs of others, and graciously says that a gift to the poor
is a loan to the Lord, who will repay with interest. At the same
time God denounces the greedy, the covetous, the opportunist who
will not sell grain or foodstuffs in a time of famine or need.

The text makes clear that hoarding or "cornering a market" is
not a new practice; many instances can be found in ancient history
of this preying upon the helpless in a time of famine or national
emergency. Even in the most civilized societies, laws are multiplied
to control the greed and rapacity of unscrupulous men, the vultures
and wolves who prey upon the weak, the old, and the defenseless.

It is true, as economists point out, that money is neither good
nor bad, but—obviously—men are. Money is simply the extension
of one's power to do good or harm. Men whose minds are corrupt
use money for all kinds of evil purposes and may with it corrupt
the minds and morals of others. Cynics say that justice always
favors the man of wealth; the poor who run afoul of the law must
pay through long imprisonment or with their lives, while "justice"
finds a way for the man of means. In the Middle Ages even church
offices were bought by the well-to-do, and some renegades who
piled up great fortunes left money to endow churches or to establish
chantries where priests on a regular schedule prayed for the repose
of the benefactor's soul. In scores of countries and cities "popular
elections" are held, but vote-buying or frauds at the polls often
make a travesty of the democratic processes. Men—and women—
will sell their honor for money, and millions in America accept the
here-and-now philosophy of Omar: "Take the cash and let the credit
go." One of the popular sayings of our time is "Money may not be
everything, but it's way ahead of whatever is second."

The Need for Stewardship

Christians, like the faithful in old Israel, have a conscience about
money. They are concerned equally about the means of acquiring
it and the handling of it. They look upon material wealth as they
do life, health, and other blessings, as a gift from God. This may
be called the sacramental view of life. Since money is an extension
of one's power, they accept it as a means—not an end—and en-
deavor to use it for advancing God's kingdom or helping those in
need. This is not to say that consecrated people do not supply their
own needs; certainly they must do this like anyone else. But they
look upon prosperity or income as a stewardship in which they
simply manage the property of another, in this case, God's. Like

the zealous Christians in the first church, the Jerusalem church, "not one of them said that aught of the things which he possessed was his own" (Acts 4:32b). They were only managers.

Stewardship is an office in which trust and responsibility are the primary requirements. God has committed his goods into trustworthy hands, and the steward is thereafter responsible for the use of the goods, whatever they may be. "Here, moreover, it is required in stewards that a man be found faithful" (1 Cor. 4:2). Eventually, God's stewards, like the stewards or trustees of a bank, a union, or a shipping company, must give an account of their stewardship.

Money, like temptation, tests a man. It makes fools of some; it makes philanthropists of others. Each of us acts according to deep-seated urges or, in some cases, principles. Those who have longed for pleasure, ease, or luxury find that money will give them the power to indulge these desires. Those who are truly benevolent find opportunities on every side to help the homeless, the aged and infirm, the calls of devoted missionaries.

This concept, involving as it does man's relationship to God the provider and to man as a needy creature (needing self-understanding and salvation as well as food and human fellowship), is the highest view of life. Thus the sacramental view of wealth, whether it is little or much, is a revolutionary philosophy whose roots are found in the prophecies and moral precepts of the Old Testament, including the book of Proverbs.

Questions

1. What do you think of the golden mean between poverty and wealth (30:8, 9)?
2. What was the commonly held view about prosperity? Is this a biblical view in any sense? Why or why not?
3. Must a man care about money and property? Why?
4. Note the exhortations to industry, thrift, and care of property. Is not all property a trust? Discuss the implications of this.
5. What important limitations did God place upon the getting of wealth?
6. What protection did the Jewish law give to the poor?
7. Why is hoarding, or the piling up of wealth, wrong?
8. Cite examples of "sharing the wealth," examples from the Scriptures or from history.
9. Discuss the necessity of Christian stewardship.
10. How may we overcome "the love of money"?

Chapter Six

SINS OF THE FLESH:
IDLENESS AND ANGER

My son, if sinners entice thee, consent thou not. Proverbs 1:10

SIN MAY BE described as anything offensive to God and harmful to man. The term sin is variously defined in the scriptures as rebellion (Deut. 9:7), transgression or flagrant disobedience (1 Sam. 15:23), missing the mark or failing (Rom. 3:23), evil desire or "reaching after pleasure" (James 1:15), and all unrighteousness (1 John 5:17).

The concept of sin is, of course, related to man's free will. Because man is free to choose among any number of alternatives and because he is conscious of his decisions and their consequences, he is responsible for his actions. Ancient as well as modern law takes into account the important element of will or purpose. For example, a man may kill his neighbor accidentally while hunting, and the act would be called manslaughter, not murder. In this case the mind and will were not involved. But to lie in wait for a person and shoot him involves hatred, intention, and a voluntary act. The Mosaic law made a sharp distinction between intentional and accidental killing. Sin, therefore, as the Sermon on the Mount clearly teaches, comes from evil in the heart (Matt. 5:21-23).

Broadly speaking, there are three types of sins: (1) offenses against God or authority, (2) offenses against men, and (3) offenses against one's own self or nature. In one sense, all wrongs are specifically directed against God's nature or will. These would include, under the Old Testament particularly, such sins as worshipping idols, violating the Lord's Sabbath, blasphemy, and any disobedience of divine law. Sins against others, whether neighbors or strangers, would include

43

acts of cruelty and violence, injustice, deceit or fraud, misrepresentation or lying, and the more subtle sins like contempt and arrogance.

In the third category may be listed such sins as indolence and sloth, gluttony, drunkenness, fornication or any abuse of the body. Filthiness of body or mind is an offense primarily against one's self, though unless one lives like the ancient hermits, in a cave or on a mountain apart, society will also be offended. When the apostle Paul warned against fornication, he argued, "Every sin that man doeth is without the body' but he that committeth fornication sinneth against his own body" (1 Cor. 6:18). He also spoke of perverted men "as abusers of themselves" (1 Cor. 6:9) who receive in their bodies "that recompense of their error which was due" (Rom. 1:27).

In this and the next chapter we shall discuss some of the sins that especially affect the life and influence of the individual. These sins may for convenience be called the sins of the flesh or personal sins; they are generally sins of excess. Two will be dealt with in this chapter: idleness and anger.

Idleness—the Sin of Irresponsibility

Idleness in small doses is not only enjoyable but beneficial. The leisure that we prize so much on holidays or vacations is pleasurable because it is a break in the daily routine of labor or responsibility. It is a little like straightening up when one has been bending over for a long time, picking strawberries or pulling grass from the flower beds. The change from work to play or recreation is good for body and mind. But this is not idleness. It is a change of scene and of activity. The very infrequency of holidays or vacations makes them precious. They are a kind of fruit earned by hard work—and even Christ, busy as he was, saw the need of this kind of change.

When the apostles came in from a journey and reported all they had been doing, the Master said, "Come ye yourselves apart into a desert place, and rest a while" (Mark 6:31). Note, however, that the labor came first, then the rest. There is no satisfaction in rest unless it has been earned. An enforced rest is often like a prison sentence.

Idleness is shirking one's duty, resting when one should be working, sleeping when the sun is high. In America, thanks to the influence of many factors, among them the teachings of the New Testament on the need of working and taking care of oneself and his family, idleness was scorned and despised (Franklin's proverbs, for example, constantly reiterated the need for hard work, thrift, and the care of property). In colonial Jamestown, Virginia, John Smith had to apply the apostle Paul's injunction, "He that will not work, neither let him eat," to get certain "gentlemen" to work.

In the Proverbs, idleness and the sluggard are roundly reproved. As an example:

> How long wilt thou sleep, O sluggard?
> When wilt thou arise out of thy sleep?
> Yet a little sleep, a little slumber,
> A little folding of the hands to sleep:
> So shall thy proverty come as a robber,
> And thy want as an armed man.
>   (6:9-11)

In this passage, which admonishes the sluggard to take a lesson in industry from the ants, the very spirit of the sluggard is caught in the language. The lazy person has been sleeping overlong and tries to justify his behavior by the repeated word "little"—"a little sleep," "a little slumber," "a little folding of the hands." But the preceptor is not impressed; this self-indulgence leads quickly to poverty and hunger. In typical fashion the Hebrew poet pictures the action and makes it dramatic. The hands that should be planting, cultivating, or doing other useful work are folded, lying at rest. And poverty comes as stealthily as a robber to steal the man's accumulated food or money. Or, in another figure, stark "want" comes like an armed man to take the sluggard's substance. The inactivity of the slothful man is set in sharp contrast against the active forces of poverty and hunger.

What is wrong with taking one's ease when all others are at work? First, it is a failure to provide for oneself or, in some instances, for one's family. The sluggard wants his share of food and the comforts of the home, but at somebody else's expense. So he shifts his burden of responsibility to others. The sluggard may be an immature son or daughter who stays in the nest because it is comfortable and he does not need to worry about the work or the bills. Or he could be, in the language of Proverbs, "a worthless person," that is, an improvident father or a lazy and useless mother. Basically the sin of idleness is its selfishness, living on the labors of others.

The results of idleness are: (1) loss of self-respect and the esteem of others, (2) poverty and hunger ("Love not sleep, lest thou come to poverty" (20:13); and (3) the loss of property.

> I went by the field of the sluggard,
> And by the vineyard of the man void of understanding
> And, lo, it was all grown over with thorn,

45

The face thereof was covered with nettles,
And the stone wall thereof was broken down.
(24:30, 31)

This depressing picture leads quite naturally to a moral lesson: "Then I beheld, and considered well; I saw, and received instructions" (24:32).

Anger—The High Road to Sin

One of the common marks of our humanity is the powerful emotion of anger or resentment. It may be defined as a strong feeling aroused by real or supposed wrong. All normal persons, evidence suggests, experience at times a deep sense of displeasure or wrath accompanied by an urge to retaliate; thus we speak of "a surge of anger." The anger may be caused by injury, injustice, misrepresentation or various other offenses against oneself or others. Since the response to threats or injury to oneself or his self-esteem is so instinctive or natural, anger cannot categorically be called wrong or sinful. Historically the term is related to the Icelandic word *angr,* sorrow or grief, and to the Germanic word *Angst,* fear or anxiety.

Several passages in the Old Testament, as all Bible students know, refer to God's anger. Two examples will suffice: (1) Moses' intercession for Israel shortly after the people had made the golden calf and God was minded to destroy them (Exodus 32:9-12), and (2) Joshua's warning to Israel in his farewell address that God's anger will be "kindled against you" if ye "serve other gods" (Joshua 23:16). It is interesting to note that, although Moses pleaded with God not to destroy the people he had delivered from Egypt, Moses himself gave way to anger a short time later (Ex. 32:19).

When Anger is Just

On one occasion Jesus is said to have been angry. The incident, recorded in Mark, tells of Christ's entering the synogogue and finding there a man with a withered hand. The crowd watched to see whether Christ would heal him, for it was a Sabbath day. When Jesus asked the man to stand up, he directed a question to the worshippers: "Is it lawful on the Sabbath day to do good, or to do harm? to save a life or to kill?" Since they could give only one reasonable answer, which would then have shown their loyalty to tradition and unconcern for the sufferer, the record says "they held their peace." "And when he had looked round about on them with anger, being grieved at the hardening of their heart, he saith unto the man, Stretch forth thy hand" (Mark 3:1-6). Two emotions of our Lord are mentioned in this passage: Compassion for the afflicted man and anger, mingled with grief, because of the blindness and hardness of the people.

Another incident, much more widely known, occurred when Jesus cast the tradesmen and moneychangers out of the Temple. But though he overturned the tables of the money-changers and drove all the merchants out of the Temple, none of the writers describes him as angry. In each report, Christ rebuked the men who thus violated the place of worship and quoted two statements from the prophets, "My house shall be called a house of prayer" and "ye make it a den of robbers" (Matt. 21:12-14). His precipitate action was undoubtedly meant to dramatize the greedy behavior of men who had capitalized on the need of the people to buy animals for the sacrifice or to exchange foreign coins so as to buy sacrifices from the traders there. Once again Jesus tried to fix attention on the spiritual, not the physical, and to show the true meaning of the Mosaic law. His impatience with these usurpers may very well have been anger, or what is often called righteous indignation. But it was not personal bitterness or wrath. As John described an earlier cleansing of the Temple, the disciples saw the Lord's conduct as zeal toward God's house (John 2:17).

We are made to recognize, therefore, that anger is not in itself evil. It often leads to intemperate language or action, or among violent persons, to violent and destructive acts. One needs to look beyond the anger to its cause. Many kinds of behavior may arouse anger or anguish in the heart of a just or pure person. If one is not angered when he sees a helpless child beaten, defrauded, or abused, something is lacking in that person's makeup. Again, to see a blind person attacked or cheated and not rise to his defense is both cowardly and unchristian. In several scriptures God is declared to be "slow to anger," merciful, gracious, and ready to forgive wrongdoing (see, for example, Ex. 34:6, 7, and Neh. 6:17ff.). In the Psalms are found many references to God's putting away his anger and forgiving the sins of Israel, e.g.:

> Thou hast forgiven the iniquity of thy people;
> Thou hast covered all their sin.
> Thou hast taken away all thy wrath;
> Thou hast turned thyself from the fierceness of thine anger.
> (Psalm 85:2,3)

The very fact that God is said to be "slow to anger" indicates that he can and will be angry when men impudently disobey him or do grave wrong to others. If God never showed anger or punished the most frightful wrongdoing, men could not respect him as good or just. His justice demands generosity and goodness to faithful and worthy men and punishment for the wicked.

Warning about Anger

Having laid down these principles about anger, let us turn to this topic in the Proverbs. The first passage pays a compliment to self-controlled persons:

> He that is slow to anger is of great understanding:
> But he that is hasty of spirit exalteth folly.
>
> (14:29)

Just a few verses further on occurs the well-known couplet:

> Righteousness exalteth a nation;
> But sin is a reproach to any people.
>
> (14:34)

There seems to be an implied connection between self-control ("slow to anger") and righteousness, as there is also between the "hasty" of spirit and sin. Another passage makes clear that

> A soft answer turneth away wrath:
> But a grievous word stirreth up anger.
>
> (15:1)

A parallel verse merely reverses the subject:

> A wrathful man stirreth up contention;
> But he that is slow to anger appeaseth strife.
>
> (15:18)

From another point of view, discretion or good judgment is said to be a check on anger:

> The discretion of a man maketh him slow to anger:
> And it is his glory to pass over a transgression.
>
> (19:11)

A comparable statement is this:

> A fool uttereth all his anger:
> But a wise man keepeth it back and stilleth it.
>
> (26:11)

It becomes apparent, as we put these various statements together, that the writer is once again drawing a distinction between the prudent or wise man and the fool. The discreet man keeps his anger and his tongue under control; the fool gives way to his wrath in abusive or violent language. Likewise, the good man, even though he may be wronged, tried by his coolness and quietness to placate the angry or intemperate man. One uses his intelligence to try to avoid or end quarrels; the other uses his hostility to provoke anger and violence in others.

In many a situation, whether in a disagreement between husband and wife, between employer and employee, or even between a patrolman and a motorist, thoughtful persons have found that "a soft answer turneth away wrath."

Finally, in a note that seems to show the utter hopelessness of the man quickly angered, the writer says:

> Seest thou a man that is hasty in his words?
> There is more hope of a fool than of him.
> (29:20)

Knowing well how the fool is regarded throughout this book, we can appreciate how low this loud-mouthed and angry man has fallen. Even the soft-headed fool can look down on him.

Questions

1. Define sin, either biblically or experientially.
2. How are sin and free will related? Can there be sin if there is no freedom of the will? Why or why not?
3. Do you find more than three categories of sin? Discuss these categories.
4. Of which sins are we, and mankind generally, most aware?
5. Why is idleness usually frowned upon by Western nations?
6. Is rest and recreation in harmony with Christ's teaching? What are its limitations?
7. How do you distinguish idleness from relaxation and quiet meditation?
8. Does modern society have any sluggards? What is the biblical answer to this problem?
9. Is anger always wrong? Can you support your position?
10. Compare the anger of most men with the incident of Christ driving the moneychangers from the temple.
11. How can anger be checked or controlled? When does it become sin?

Chapter Seven

SINS OF THE FLESH:
GLUTTONY AND DRUNKENNESS

Who hath woe? Who hath sorrow? Who hath contentions?
They that tarry long at the wine . . . . (Proverbs 23:29)

THE LAND OF Palestine was famous in ancient times for its fruit-fulness and particularly for its grapes. The story of the spies who brought out the immense cluster of grapes, symbolic of the land's productivity, is well known (Num. 13:23, 24). Wine was one of the chief products of the country throughout its history and was naturally associated with the affluent life. One of the prophecies used to suggest an abundant life is the passage declaring "they shall sit every man under his vine and fig tree . . ." (Micah 4:4). In several Old Testament books Israel is compared to a fruitful vine planted in a fertile field (see, for example, Isa. 5:1-7; Psalms 80:8-11, and Jer. 12:10).

Wine was used in sacrifices and offerings, both in the worship of God (Num. 28:14) and to false gods (Deut. 32:27-33, Isa. 57:6). In Judges 9:13, wine is described as that "which cheereth God and man." In metaphorical passages wine is used to represent abundance and goodness.

Attitudes Toward Wine

In both the Old and the New Testament, wine is praised and condemned. Its use among the people was common; it was taken with meals, and it came to be used with many religious rituals, particularly with the Passover in the post-exilic age.

50

The first mention of wine culture is given in Genesis in connection with Noah's drunkenness and exposure (Gen. 9:20-27). Various prophets condemn the use or misuse of wine (Isa. 5:11, Hab. 2:5). Isaiah condemns those priests who "reel and stagger" (Isa. 28:7). Daniel refused the king's dainties and his wine and yet, after the test he proposed, looked better and stronger than those who partook of the king's fare (Dan. 1:5, 8, 15).

The Nazarites, probably because they had witnessed the luxury and debauchery of the Canaanites, took vows never to drink wine or use any product of the vine (Judges 13:4, 7). The Old Testament book which most clearly condemns the immoderate use of wine is Proverbs.

Yet in the Psalms David thanks God for wine "that maketh glad the heart of man" (Psalm 104:15). In this setting it is listed among his good gifts to man.

In the New Testament, John the Baptist took no wine and was thus considered by some to have a demon (Luke 7:33). Jesus, who came "eating and drinking," was called "a winebibber and a friend of publicans and sinners" (Luke 7:34).

In ancient times, wine was taken with meals, served on feast days, at weddings, at homecomings, for the enjoyment of guests (consider the account of the wedding Jesus attended, John 2:1-10). The wine which Jesus provided, after the host's supply had been exhausted, was described as better than the first.

The literature of the rabbis indicates that wine was commonly used as a medicine for various types of stomach and intestinal disorders (note the reference to keeping wine, Luke 5:37-39). The Samaritan who found the wounded man beside the road "bound up his wounds, pouring in them oil and wine" and "took care of him" (Luke 10:34). In addition, wine was often taken, not as a stimulant, but as a relaxant. Paul's advice to Timothy—"take no longer water, but use a little wine for thy stomach's sake and thine often infirmities"—has been quoted with warm appreciation by many generations. Before the advent of modern medicine, doctors frequently used wine or strong drink for a variety of ills, including its use as an opiate to deaden pain. Its use among wounded soldiers is a matter of record. Sometimes large quantities of alcohol were given to drug the senses before an operation was performed. Today, of course, more effective medicines and opiates are available in most parts of the world.

Christian men and women are exhorted not to be "given to much wine" (1 Tim. 3:2, 3, 8, 11) but to be "temperate and sober-minded" (see also Titus 2:1-3). It is evident that Christians in Corinth showed lack of proper respect for the Lord's supper by eating and drinking for their own satisfaction and even becoming drunken (1 Cor. 11:20, 21). Thus, in correcting this abuse, the apostle asked, "What, have ye not houses to eat and to drink in?"

Misuse of Wine

One of the weaknesses of the flesh mentioned but not dwelt on in the Proverbs is that of winebibbing or drinking to excess. In several of the prophetic books this evil is depicted in more detail and held up as a national shame. For example, a passage in Isaiah shows the low state of Israel, God's chosen people:

> Woe unto them that rise up early in the morning, that they may follow strong drink; that tarry late into the night, till wine inflame them! And the harp and the lute, the tabret and the pipe and wine, are in their feasts; but they regard not the work of Jehovah . . . (Isaiah 5:11, 12)

Another passage in Isaiah condemns the sins of Ephraim, saying "the crown of pride of the drunkards of Ephraim shall be trodden under foot." Even the religious leaders are guilty of drunkenness:

> And even these reel with wine and stagger with strong drink; the priest and the prophet reel with strong drink, they are swallowed up of wine, they stagger with strong drink; they err in vision, they stumble in judgment. (Isaiah 28:7)

Another interesting note is found in this description of wine in Habakkuk:

> Yea, moreover, wine is treacherous, a haughty man, that keepeth not at home; who enlargeth his desire as Sheol, and he is as death, and cannot be satisfied, but gathered unto him all nations, and heapeth unto him all peoples.
> (Habakkuk 2:5)

From reading these statements, we learn that wine and strong drink are troublesome: strong drink is said to "inflame" men, to turn their minds "away from the work of Jehovah," to make men "reel" and "stagger," to "err in vision," to "stumble in judgment." It is a "mocker," deceiving or deluding men and causing them to lose self-control, to make mistaken judgments, and to behave in irresponsible ways.

Consider now the fullest treatment of this topic in the Proverbs:

> Who hath woe? Who hath sorrow? Who hath contentions?
> Who hath complaining? Who hath wounds without cause?
> Who hath redness of eyes?

They that tarry long at the wine;
They that go to seek out mixed wine.
(23:20-30)

Here the effects of strong drink are graphically described. Then the more serious problem of continued use is figuratively set forth:

At the last it biteth like a serpent,
And stingeth like an adder.
(23:32)

The series of questions which opens this passage draws attention to the physical effects of drinking. The social and moral consequences are compared to the sting of a deadly serpent. Some of the further problems of drink are cited:

Thine eyes shall behold strange things,
Thy heart shall utter perverse things.
Yea, thou shalt be as he that lieth down in the midst of the sea,
Or as he that lieth upon the top of a mast.
They have stricken me, shalt thou say, and I was not hurt:
They have beaten me, and I felt it not:
When shall I awake? I will seek it yet again.
(23:33-35)

Even a modern writer describing the drunken behavior of a man could hardly make the picture more realistic. Vision has been blurred, the mind befogged, the mouth speaks evil or "perverse" things, and the victim endangers his life by lying down in dangerous places. Furthermore, he is confused, accusing others of having beaten him; and when he sobers up, he begins to seek again for the stupefying drink. Thus drink robs a man of his reason and his self-control. In this dangerous state he is likely to do things that he would not ever do when sober, and he is likely to hurt himself and others.

Another passage indicates some of the motivations for drinking:

It is not for kings, O Lemuel, it is not for kings to drink wine;
Nor for princes to say, Where is strong drink?
Lest they drink and forget the law,
And pervert the justice due to any that is afflicted.
Give strong drink unto him that is ready to perish,
And wine unto the bitter in soul:
Let him drink, and forget his poverty,
And remember his misery no more.
(31:4-7)

Here is the first clear indication that even in Solomon's day drink was considered an opiate. Men drank for many reasons, but some drank "to forget," to escape from the tedium or bitterness of life. Men who face overwhelming problems, or who cannot cope with life, have often tried to bolster their confidence or to escape, at least for a time, by resorting to the oblivion of alcohol.

In the passage just quoted the king is strongly urged not to fall victim to the deadening influence of alcohol lest he "forget the law" and "pervert justice." As the lawgiver and judge, he must keep his mind clear and mete out judgments fairly and righteously (see verses 8 and 9 of this chapter).

Proverbs provides ample warning against the evils of strong drink. But it also supplements these warnings with exhortations to avoid another kind of self-indulgence: gluttony.

Gluttony

By general agreement, the enjoyment of food is one of life's best and most common pleasures. Good food, well prepared, is not only one of man's necessities; it is also one of his weaknesses. In ancient times the search for food was a chief occupation of the tribe or clan; and quite often, as many primitive tribes today, there might be days of feasting followed by long periods of near-famine. Providing the daily bread or meat for oneself or family has been, in all ages, one of the chief responsibilities of men. Making bread and preparing meat for the family table has traditionally been one of the most important tasks of women (Prov. 31:14, 15).

The enjoyment of fellowship is one of the reasons why, in hospitable homes, relatives and guests are always welcome. Even the word company (or companion) bears witness to the ancient sharing of food, for the term comes from the Latin and means to eat together or break bread together. In the homes of rich and poor alike the act of sharing meals with visitors or friends is a time-honored way of showing love (see Heb. 13:1-2).

Bible students will remember the generosity of the early Christians in the Jerusalem church who freely opened their homes to the converts who were far from home (Acts 2:43-45). Apparently the churches in the apostolic time had a love feast (*agape*) which usually preceded the Lord's supper, but in the Corinthian church (divided already into several parties) these meals were not occasions of joy, peace, and sharing but showed instead the selfishness and division of the congregation. Thus Paul (1 Cor. 11:17-22) rebukes them for their lack of love and their divisive spirit. Instead of sharing a common meal, "each one taketh his own supper, and one is hungry, and another is drunken." Some had much while others had very little and "were put to shame." By this kind of discrimination the believers in

Corinth showed a shocking disregard for what was originally a "love feast." A social event had lost it sociableness and become a parody of Christian unity.

The Lack of Control

In the Proverbs are several passages dealing with the sin of of gluttony. Two of these are found in chapter twenty-three:

> When thou sittest to eat with a ruler,
> Consider diligently him [footnote, *what*] that is before thee;
> And put a knife to thy throat,
> If thou be a man given to appetite
> Be not desirous of his dainties;
> Seeing they are deceitful food.
> (23:1-3)

The expression "a knife to thy throat" is an Eastern figure for self-control or restraint. The man "given to appetite," faced with the temptations offered by the king's table, must know more than etiquette and social graces. He must know when to say "enough." In ancient times such dinners were occasions for the ruler or rich man to impress his guests with the luxury and variety of food and drink he could afford, in other words, a chance to display his vanity. For the guest it was often an occasion for gorging.

The "man given to appetite" is one who lives to eat. Not content with what the writer of Proverbs calls "the food that is needful" (30:8), the gluttonous man eats at one sitting enough for two or three hearty men. Sometimes he takes pride in his ability "to put it away" and tries to eat everything on the table, even though his more restrained companions have long since given up the unequal contest. Such a man is an offense to his host and an embarrassment to his family. But he goes on eating and drinking, as oblivious of the other diners as Dr. Samuel Johnson often was.

Gluttony is one of the sins of excess. Of course, in modern society the terms "glutton" and "gluttony" are seldom heard; instead, we gloss over the evil practice by calling it "overeating" or "eating too well." The sin of gluttony, whatever it is called, is rooted in selfishness, it is a half-brother to avarice, and is a panderer to lechery. An old Jewish writer declares, "Sumptuous nourishment excites to wanton debauchery." Chaucer, in the "Pardoner's Tale," declares:

> To kindle and blow the fire of lechery
> That is annexed unto gluttony.

Some pithy or proverbial expressions show the need for controlling the desire for food. Benjamin Franklin gave us the saying of Poor Richard—"To lengthen thy life, lessen thy meals." Thomas Jefferson said that "we never repent of having eaten too little." And Ovid, one of the Roman contemporaries of Christ, advised, "Stop short of your appetite; eat less than you are able." Another writer states, "The fool who eats till he is sick must fast till he is well." In a lighter vein a modern maxim says, "If you wish to grow thinner, diminish your dinner."

Any kind of excess is hurtful and wrong. Even what is good and legitimate can be harmful when the appetites are not controlled. Even the lower animals seem to recognize and follow this principle, though some, like human beings, do not know when to stop and eat until they burst. In the Golden Age of Greece, the temple of Apollo at Delphi had engraved on it "Nothing too much." Thus the answer to overeating, or to any excess, is self-control. "The root of all morality," wrote Fichte, "is self-control." And one of the old Jewish sayings is still true: "Moderation prolongs life."

A second passage in Proverbs reinforces this teaching:

Hast thou found honey? eat so much as is sufficient for thee,
Lest thou be filled therewith, and vomit it.

All of us have seen signs in cafeterias and children's camps which admonished, "Eat as much as you want, but take no more than you want." Some of us had parents who reproved the over-zealous child when he took more than he could eat, "Ah, I see that your eyes are bigger than your stomach." Sometimes, to teach an object lesson, they would save the plateful of food to the next meal and set it before the big-eyed youngster.

To refined persons the term gluttony is offensive. It suggests the behavior of animals, wolfing their food as if it might be grabbed by another and there would not be enough to go around. Wild animals, and sometimes dogs, quarrel over their food and try to drive off any possible rival while they gobble down everything in sight. They are greedy, impatient, and anti-social.

Christians are taught to exercise control in all things; as the apostle advised, "Let your moderation be known unto all men." (Phil. 4:5 KJV) In another letter the same writer, giving instruction about the relative unimportance of meats in relation to one's spiritual welfare, declares that a true Christian should be willing even to give up meat rather than cause another to sin. Then he adds, significantly, "for the kingdom of God is not eating and drinking, but righteousness and peace and joy in the Holy Spirit" (Rom. 14:17).

Both drunkenness and gluttony are allied sins: they are sins of excess and self-indulgence. Strong drink and an excess of food are evils to be avoided. The Christian's attitude is well summed up in the apostle Paul's admonition, "Don't get your stimulus from wine (for there is always the danger of excessive drinking), but let the Spirit stimulate your souls" (Eph. 5:18, Phillips).

Questions

1. What is the Bible's attitude toward strong drink?
2. List some of the evils of drunkenness.
3. Discuss both the physical and spiritual effects of strong drink.
4. What are some of the motivations people give for drinking? What is the Bible's response to these?
5. What is the origin of the word companion?
6. Why do we generally use euphemisms for the sin of gluttony?
7. Which is worse, drunkenness or gluttony? Defend your answer.
8. Is there a relationship between lust and overeating? Discuss.
9. What is the root of morality?
10. What is Christ's teaching about self-indulgence?

Chapter Eight

SINS OF THE FLESH: ADULTERY

For the lips of a strange woman drop honey,
And her mouth is smoother than oil:
But in the end she is bitter as wormwood,
Sharp as a two-edged sword. Proverbs 5:3, 4

SOMEONE HAS SAID that if a young man would take to heart the warnings and prohibitions found in the Proverbs and add to these the qualities of life set forth in the Sermon on the Mount, he would be a near-perfect man. In Proverbs the sins of the flesh—gluttony, wine-bibbing, and fornication—are presented in graphic detail, and the warnings are clear and specific.

The wiles of the "foolish woman" or harlot are discussed in several long passages in chapters two to nine. It is significant that each chapter, from two to eight, begins with an admonition addressed to "my son" or "my sons" to heed the father's advice and reject the temptations to sin. Chapter four, for example, begins as follows:

Hear, my sons, the instruction of a father,
And attend to know understanding:
For I give you good doctrine;
Forsake ye not my law.

Then the writer refers to having learned these precepts from his father, who likewise counseled against disobedience and fleshly indulgence. In persuasive language the writer urges the son to love wisdom and understanding and the ways of uprightness. In particular the young are urged to follow instruction: "enter not into the path of the wicked," "walk not in the way of evil men," and "make level the path of thy feet" that "all thy ways may be established." One particularly memorable passage in this chapter emphasizes the conscience:

> Keep thy heart with all diligence;
> For out of it are the issues of life.
> (4:23)

Although the structure of the book of Proverbs is often difficult to understand, the use of contrast is especially prominent; here it is seen in the beauties and rewards of wisdom (a life lived in harmony with God's will) presented immediately before the description of the scarlet woman (whose attractions are false and whose effect is destructive). Certainly the contrast between these two allurements is not accidental.

The Ways of the Wicked

Chapters three and four have extolled wisdom and described her gracious rewards. Then chapter five, after repeating the injunction to "attend unto my wisdom," moves quickly to a description of the "strange woman" whose honied words and deceitful ways lure the unwary on to death.

> In the end she is bitter as wormwood,
> Sharp as a two-edged sword.
> Her feet go down to death;
> Her steps take hold on Sheol.
> (5:4, 5)

The young man must make his choice; he cannot love wisdom (the way of righteousness) and at the same time lust after the evil woman, whose ways lead to dishonor and death.

> His own iniquities shall take the wicked,
> And he shall be holden with the cords of his sin.
> He shall die for lack of instruction;
> And in the greatness of his folly he shall go astray.
> (5:22, 23)

Since man's nature is the same in all places and in all ages, the descriptions of the harlot's lures and the young man's inclination are as pertinent today as when Solomon wrote them. Flattery or "fair speech" is one of the lures of the evil woman:

> Come, let us take our fill of love until the morning;
> Let us solace ourselves with loves.
> For the man is not at home;
> He is gone on a long journey.

With her much fair speech she causeth him to yield;
With the flattering of her lips she forces him along,
                    (7:18, 19, 21)

The woman of pleasure is bold, "wily of heart," and wilful. Having cast off her natural modesty, she walks the streets, frequents the public places, and seeks out these willing victims "void of understanding." One of her devices is the quite familiar appeal

Stolen waters are sweet
And bread eaten in secret is pleasant.
                    (9:17)

To the young, in particular, this is a powerful attraction, for in addition to the thrill of a forbidden experience, there is the fillip of danger. The secret meeting at night, the sense of escaping detection and of gratifying the flesh and exercising one's freedom all make the experience an adventure.

The scarlet woman is impudent and aggressive, lying in wait "at every corner."

So she caught him and kissed him,
And with an impudent face she said unto him:
Sacrifices of peace offering are with me:
This day have I paid my vows.
Therefore came I forth to meet thee,
Diligently to seek thy face, and I have found thee.
                    (7:13-15)

Though she is public property, she gives the youthful victim the feeling that she has come seeking "thy face" — and he believes and follows her.

He goeth after her straightway,
As an ox goeth to the slaughter,
Or as one in fetters to the correction of the fool
Till an arrow strike through his liver;
As a bird hasteth to the snare,
And knoweth not it is for his life.
                    (7:22-23)

A false or painted beauty is one of the marks of the harlot.

Lust not after her beauty in thy heart;
Neither let her take thee with her eyelids.
                    (6:25)

Lust begins in the eye, as the experience of King David who looked upon Bathsheba bathing clearly shows (2 Sam. 11:2ff.) and as Christ emphasized in the Sermon on the Mount:

> Ye have heard that it was said, Thou shalt
> not commit adultery: but I say unto you
> that everyone that looketh on a woman to
> lust after her hath committed adultery with
> her already in his heart.
>
> (Matt. 5:27-28)

In a similar vein the apostle Peter describes a class of men as "having eyes full of adultery" (or as the original puts it, "an adulteress") "and that cannot cease from sin" (2 Peter 2:14).

In the past ages the dress, the painted face, the loose speech and bold behavior proclaimed the woman of the streets. In more recent times the styles of dress and the immodesty of many worldly women have blurred the distinction between the decent and the common woman. There is no denying that low-cut and tight-fitting dresses, as well as loose speech and immodest behavior, have encouraged men to make improper advances. Thus, beyond any doubt, many women have provoked lust and emboldened men—whether this was their intention or not.

Sinning Against Oneself and Others

More attention in the proverbs is given to the consequences of lust than to describing the wiles of the harlot. In the pictorial language of Hebrew poetry the effects of sin are graphically stated:

> For on account of a harlot a man is brought
> to a piece of bread.   (6:26a)

Moreover, the lack of justification for such a sin is also made clear:

> Men do not despise a thief, if he steal
> To satisfy himself when he is hungry;
>
> He that committeth adultery with a woman is
> void of understanding;
> He doeth it who would destroy his own soul.
>
> (6:30, 32)

Besides the moral wrong involved, adultery with a married woman was an open violation of the strict Jewish law and punishable by death (Lev. 20:10). Thus by sinning against a neighbor and his family, a foolish man would open a Pandora's box of troubles.

So he that goeth in to his neighbor's wife;
Whoever touches her shall not be unpunished.
(6:29)

Wounds and dishonor shall he get:
And his reproach shall not be wiped away.
For jealousy is the rage of a man;
And he will not spare in the day of vengeance.
He will not regard any ransom;
Neither will he rest content, though thou
    givest many gifts.
(6:33-35)

In the Mosaic law or Decalogue, the seventh commandment, "Thou shalt not commit adultery," stands between the law against killing and the law forbidding stealing. Adultery is clearly related to both killing and stealing. When a man cohabits with another's wife, he destroys the woman's virtue and her good name while by the same act he alienates the woman's love for her husband; these sinful acts all have the effect of killing what was once virtuous and beautiful in the relation of husband and wife. The wronged man has been robbed of something which money, time, and words of contrition cannot restore. Thus adultery, since it strikes at the roots of human relationships, is a complicated, subtle, and deeply disturbing evil.

On another level, adultery is insidious, for after the wife has once yielded and the walls have been breached, the chief defense against sinning has been removed. Logically, there is no good reason, she may argue, for refusing a second and a third illicit affair, and she becomes caught in a web of rationalizations. If she should want to demur or even give up her wrongdoing, her partner in sin will remind her that there is no reason now to quit. The self-excusing attitude of the woman is expressed in the words:

So is the way of an adulterous woman;
She eateth and wipeth her mouth,
And saith, I have done no wickedness.
(20:30)

Thus she treats her immorality as nothing more than a meal, and with a swipe of her hand she dismisses any thought of wrongdoing.

Even though both the adulterers should take this cavalier view of their behavior, the flesh and the heart cannot so lightly forget the wrong. The man has sinned against his own flesh, against the wife of another, and against the woman's husband. In a larger sense the aggressor has sinned against the community, since he has wronged a man's family and violated, whether openly or covertly, the sacredness of marriage. He has contributed to the weakening and perhaps the destruction of a home, and even if society should be so corrupt as to wink at this behavior, the moral foundations of society have been weakened.

Why Adultery is Wrong

Adultery is wrong because it is both lawless and loveless. It violates God's established order which indissolubly joins two persons for life (Matt. 19:5). Marriage was intended to give permanence and divine sanction to a union freely entered by both parties. Mutual love and trust are the foundation for a happy and lasting relationship, but adultery on the part of either man or wife breaks this bond and destroys the faith on which the marriage was founded. Adultery, therefore, undermines the home, alienates the wronged party, brings guilt and shame to the wrongdoer, and violates the moral teachings of God.

One of the tragic consequences of illicit passion is the guilt which it brings to the offender. No amount of rationalizing can clear the conscience of the guilty person, even though he may succeed in covering the sin from the eyes of others. It is common knowledge today that violating one's own moral code has disastrous effects on the personality and sets up conflicts which often result in ill health and lead to physical or nervous breakdowns. Psychologists know the sad effects of unresolved guilt upon persons: moodiness, loss of sleep and peace of mind, fear, a sense of worthlessness, and sometimes utter despair. Every violation of the moral law brings its own punishment, as philosophers have pointed out in all ages. The guilty can have no peace, as David's song of contrition (Psalm 51) clearly shows.

Adultery is also wrong because it is loveless. It is based, not on love, but on lust. Love seeks the good of the one loved; it is kind, gentle, loyal, and unselfish. But lust is self-centered, base, unsettled, seeking always its own advantage. Love protects and ennobles. Lust exploits, takes what it wants, and then rejects the object of its passion. The basic evil in lust (and therefore in adultery) is that it treats persons as things, to be used or manipulated and then cast aside. It seeks no lasting attachment; it is interested only in the flesh, and it rejects all responsibility for its behavior. Lust is like theft: the thief takes what he wants without regard to the rights or claims of others. The man who has his way with a woman is then ready to cast her off. This theme of exploitation and irresponsibility recurs again and again in literature—in Flaubert, Balzac,

Hardy, Melville, and Dreiser, to cite a few examples. Finally, lust is like a fire, raging and destructive, while love is like the rain, gentle and fructifying.

The Higher Morality

Some critics of the teaching in Proverbs have pointed out that most of the penalties mentioned in connection with adultery are only physical or social and that the reasons for avoiding this sin are mainly prudential: the adulterer is foolish, he wastes his substance and weakens his body, he is brutish and hardheaded, and he may have to deal with an enraged husband. It is true that the reasons given in this book are not so ethical or compelling as the teaching of Christ, but the contrast only emphasizes the very high moral standards of the "perfect law of liberty."

But some of the warnings are worth noting. One in particular is memorable:

> Can a man take fire in his bosom,
> And his clothes not be burned?
> Or can he walk upon hot coals,
> And his feet not be scorched?
> (6:27, 28)

Then the writer makes the application:

> So he that goeth in to his neighbor's wife;
> Whosoever toucheth her shall not be unpunished.
> (6:29)

Our modern version of this proverb is "You can't play with fire without getting burned."

Another reference speaks of a man's losing his honor and suffering, finally, in his flesh:

> Remove thy way far from her,
> And come not nigh the door of her house;
> Lest thou give thine honor unto others,
> And thy years unto the cruel;
> Lest strangers be filled with thy strength,
>
> And thou mourn at thy latter end,
> When thy flesh and thy body are consumed. . .
> (5:8-11)

One of the clearest statements to be found in Proverbs is this answer to the question "For why shouldest thou, my son, be ravished with a strange woman?"

His own iniquities shall take the wicked,
And he shall be holden with the cords of his sin.
He shall die for lack of instruction;
And in the greatness of his folly he shall go astray.
(5:22, 23)

And a final admonition—from father to son—concludes this topic:

Let not thy heart decline to her ways;
Go not astray in her paths.
For she hath cast down many wounded:
Yea, all her slain are a mighty host.
Her house is the way to Sheol,
Going down to the chambers of death.
(7:25-27)

Advice to the Married

There is another side to this picture, a side that has often been overlooked. In the midst of the many warnings about adultery, near the close of chapter five, some positive counsel is given to both husband and wife. In brief, the king's son is advised to enjoy his own youthful wife and to avoid all "foreign" entanglements:

Drink water out of thine own cistern,
And running waters our of thine own well.
Should thy springs be dispersed abroad,
And thy streams of water in the streets?
Let them be for thyself alone,
And not for strangers with thee.
Let thy fountain be blessed;
And rejoice in the wife of thy youth.
(5:15-18)

Two observations should be made about this passage: (1) this counsel is given to a married man, (2) the union is monogamous. A double responsibility is involved in the marriage relationship, as this passage shows. The husband is to find his satisfaction at home (see verse 19), and not to give his love to some "strange woman." This fact is stated quite persuasively. At the same time, the wife must gladly accept her part of the bargain or the husband will find justification for seeking love outside the home. The writer of Proverbs frankly recognizes that man will seek sexual gratification—if not at home, then elsewhere. And though he urges the husband to "rejoice in the wife of thy youth," the woman he has chosen as his companion, it follows that the wife must give him *cause* to rejoice in her love. Coldness or indifference toward her husband, constant

65

criticism of his ways or habits, and either irritability or prolonged illness can drive a man from the marriage bed. A sensitive and responsive wife will be aware of her husband's desires and needs and will do her part to make the marriage a satisfying one.

This mutual give-and-take is made more clear in the directions Paul gave to married couples:

> But because of fornications, let each man have his own wife, and let each woman have her own husband. Let the husband render unto the wife her due: and likewise also the wife unto the husband. The wife hath not power over her own body, but the husband: and likewise also the husband hath not power over his own body, but the wife. Defraud ye not one another, except it be by concent for a season . . . and [ye] may be together again, that Satan tempt you not because of your incontinency. (1 Cor. 7:2-5)

Although Paul the apostle deliberately chose the celibate life that he might serve God more freely, he recognized the rights of others to marry and accordingly gave some quite specific teaching on what husbands and wives owe to each other. When this teaching is followed faithfully, there should be harmony in the marriage and peace in the home.

Questions

1. What is the tone of the advice given about the evil woman?
2. What are the lures used by the evil woman?
3. Why is this temptation especially strong?
4. Why is the man who succumbs to adultery like an animal caught in a trap?
5. What safeguards are offered against this sin?
6. How may one recognize a common woman? What do these characteristics, therefore, say to honest and chaste women?
7. What causes the callousness of the woman after she has committed the sin of adultery?
8. How is this sin related to the sixth and eighth commandments?
9. What are the strongest arguments against adultery?
10. Compare and contrast the moral teaching of Proverbs on this subject with the standards given explicitly in the New Testament.

Chapter Nine

HUMOR

It is better to live in a corner of the housetop than in a house shared with a contentious woman. Proverbs 21:9

THOUGH THE tone of Proverbs, generally speaking, is serious and sententious, the book is enlivened by occasional passages of humor. It is a quiet, often wry, sort of humor based commonly on incongruity or shrewd observations on the behavior of eccentrics. Those persons—men or women—who depart from the norm or who exceed the bounds of common sense or engage in excesses are made to appear ridiculous. Even the humorous touches have a moral purpose, for the types or characters singled out for their odd or unsocial behavior might, presumably, be shamed or laughed into reformation. One of the aims of comic writing in ancient as well as modern periods has been to make vice or excess ridiculous and therefore not respectable in society. Under most comic sketches, therefore, the reforming spirit can be seen.

Five distinct "character" types (this term seems appropriate in view of the fact that there are no individualized portraits) are found in the book. These include: (1) the fool (native to all societies), (2) the sluggard (who avoids any activity more strenuous than eating), (3) the sharp bargainer (who belittles the seller's product until it is in the buyer's possession), (4) the windy braggart, (5) and the shrewish wife. In keeping with the style of the book, the descriptions are brief and more suggestive than explicit. Much is left to the reader's imagination or experience, but the *type* is sketched clearly enough to convey the message. Human pride and pretension, greed and weakness, are subjected to sharp ridicule.

The Fool

Whether Israel had more than its quota of fools we have no way of knowing, but the repeated references to fools and their ways would lead us to think so. This type is rash, impudent, hardheaded, careless, thoughtless, and, apparently, hopeless. They bungle everything. Even their speech arouses disgust. For example, when the fool attempts to teach or to use a parable, his effort is futile:

> The legs of the lame hang loose;
> So is a parable in the mouth of a fool.
> (26:7)

Such a comparison draws attention to the weakness and ineffectiveness of the fool's attempt to speak soberly. In another simile the same topic is touched on, but the effect of the speech is described as painful:

> As a thorn that goeth up into the hand of a drunkard,
> So is a parable in the mouth of fools.
> (26:9)

Those receiving instruction (including, of course, all who read the Proverbs) are warned, wisely enough:

> Answer not a fool according to his folly,
> Lest thou be like unto him.
> (26:4)

Then the uselessness of trying to answer the fool is suggested in the words:

> If a wise man hath a controversy with a foolish man,
> Whether he be angry or laugh, there will be no rest.
> (29:9)

We may take this to mean that there is no way to satisfy or to squelch the fool; he continues to pursue and harass the serious-minded man. So much for the speech of fools.

In the fourth section of Proverbs (chapters twenty-five through twenty-nine, a section attributed to Solomon) the conduct of fools receives much attention. How may the fool be curbed? Here is the wise man's answer:

> A whip for the horse, a bridle for the ass,
> and a rod for the back of fools.
> (26:3)

Since reason will not affect the stubborn and doltish man, then he must be treated like the animals—whipped into line. Until he learns self-control and listens to reason, he must be curbed by physical punishment. The humor in such a passage is caustic, but the likening of the fool to the horse and ass does have a certain fitness.

A more comic and imaginative figure puts the fool in an oversized mortar and attempts to extract his foolishness:

> Though than shouldest bray a fool in a mortar with a
> pestle along with bruised grain,
> Yet will not his foolishness depart from him.
>   (27:22)

Exaggeration or hyperbole is employed quite effectively here, and the mind enjoys the spectacle of a fool being brayed with a pestle. But, alas, the effort fails and the fool carries on as usual.

The Sluggard

Another generalized type, the sluggard, provides some very wry touches of humor. Characteristically, the sluggard seeks to avoid any kind of exertion; he is addicted to sleep and the soft life. Though other men go about their work, the sluggard stays indoors and cries,

> There is a lion without;
> I shall be slain in the streets.
>   (22:13, also 26:13)

Although the reference is extremely brief, the materials are present in this passage to suggest to the imagination an overweight, lazy, procrastinating drone, who has nevertheless one attractive quality— his vivid dramatic sense. A novelist or playwright could easily clothe this clever rascal in appropriate dress and make him a delightful comic figure.

The indolence of the drone is aptly described in these verses:

> As the door turneth upon its hinges,
> So doth the sluggard upon his bed.
>   (26:14)

Does not the writer subtly suggest here that as the door remains fixed upon its hinges, the dull and listless sluggard continues to turn upon his bed? He is content to take life lying down. He fears work as he does a lion roaming in the streets, and so takes the safe course of staying in bed. Immediately after the reference to the bed, the text shows the sluggard at his favorite exercise:

> The sluggard burieth his hand in the dish;
> It wearieth him to bring it again to his mouth.
>   (26:15)

Both the greediness and the laziness of the subject are spotlighted in this passage, and the reader forms his own opinion of a person who is too lazy to eat. Such little vignettes stand out starkly in the book of Proverbs because of the constant references to early rising, hard work, and the need for caring for fields and flocks. For obvious reasons the irresponsible drone was an offense to his neighbors and particularly to his teachers. Like the fool, the sluggard was the example of what a man ought not to be. Still, the tone of the references is satiric, not blunt and didactic as the passages are which deal with adultery, theft, and drunkenness. The ancient Jewish teachers were evidently aware of the values of exaggeration, irony, and wry humor in putting over their lessons.

The Hard Bargainer

A third character type, probably too well known even in Solomon's day, was the hard-driving bargainer:

It is bad, it is bad, saith the buyer;
But when he has gone his way, then he boasteth.
(20:14)

One can readily visualize the bearded buyer decrying the object offered to him, pointing out its alleged flaws, and haggling to run the price down; then, after he is safely out of hearing, gloating over his buy. The type is quite familiar. Perhaps for this reason the writer does not give more details; the brief sketch will call to mind the reader's own experiences.

Windy Clouds

The braggart is another suitable subject for humorous gibes. If the sluggard is known for his laziness, the braggart is known for his windiness. He tries to impress others by a torrent of words or by glorifying his own lackluster achievements.

As clouds and wind without rain,
So is he that boasteth himself of his gifts falsely.
(25:14)

How clearly this figure pictures the emptiness of the braggart's speech; it is like puffy clouds filled with wind but carrying no rain. In the New Testament, Jude refers to evil men in the church as "clouds without water, carried along by winds"—probably an echo of the verse cited above. The swelling clouds of summer suggest quite well the swollen language of the boaster. This kind of deception, like the buyer's disdain of the product he is trying to buy, is ludicrous because not many persons are taken in by it. The braggart, whether boasting of himself or something he owns, succeeds mainly in deceiving himself and before long he finds that his reputation goes before him. Thus in seeking to impress his neighbors, he more often only amuses them.

A similar proverb, antithetic in structure, shows clearly that men can see through the boaster's pretensions:

> Better is he that is lightly esteemed, and hath a servant,
> Than he that honoreth himself, and lacketh bread.
> (12:9)

Self-approbation is reproved in a number of instances (e.g., 26:16, 27:2), yet in the citation just quoted the contrast between the man who, though not acknowledged as powerful still has a servant, and the man who gives himself great airs and yet lacks daily bread is ludicrous. Boasting, therefore, is the defense of the weak.

The Nagging Wife

The final comic type, the nagging and contentious wife, is described with feeling. Since there are five references to this unhappy character, we may assume either that she was at least fairly well known or that Solomon had had some bad experiences with women. It is interesting that a foolish son and a troublesome wife are mentioned in the same passage:

> A foolish son is the calamity of his father;
> And the contentions of a wife are a continual dropping.
> (19:13)

As if to clarify the similitude, another proverb states that

> A continual dropping in a very rainy day
> And a contentious woman are alike.
> He that would restrain her restraineth the wind. . . .
> (27:15-16a)

The drip, drip, drip of water in a room during a heavy rain can neither be stopped nor ignored, and thus it causes tension. This continual dropping is most appropriately compared to the constant complaining or faultfinding of a woman who can no more be restrained than the wind that buffets the house. The only way to meet such a problem would seem to be to go to sleep, in the midst of the storm, or to retreat.

71

The latter course is the one suggested in another passage:

> It is better to dwell in the corner of the housetop,
> Than with a contentious woman in a wide house.
> (21:9; 25:24)

Perhaps there has been a change in the weather, and the vexed husband finds a little peace on the housetop. Yet the passage suggests that he may make that his permanent habitation, since even a large house does not give room enough to escape the barks of the critic. A little later, in the same chapter, we find that the man has fled from her presence:

> It is better to dwell in a desert land,
> Than with a contentious and fretful woman.
> (21:19)

One other sharp reference to women (who, nevertheless, seem to come off far better than men) is found in chapter eleven:

> As a ring of gold in a swine's snout,
> So is a fair woman that is without discretion.
> (11:22)

The humor here is based on incongruity—the supposed putting of a precious and beautiful gold ring in a hog's nose. When one realizes the esteem in which the Jews held gold and their utter contempt for swine, this joining of the two is most forceful. So an attractive woman is hopelessly marred by a want of good judgment.

By modern standards the humor in Proverbs may seem rather dry and strained. It is never hilarious or wildly comic (who would expect it to be in the Bible?), but is often sly, even subtle, and dependent mainly upon contrast, incongruity, and comic suggestion.

Questions

1. Name the five character types described in Proverbs.
2. How are fools to be treated?
3. What are the characteristics of the sluggard?
4. How do sluggards live today?
5. What effective figure is used to describe the braggart?
6. What can a man do about a contentious woman?
7. To what is a woman without discretion compared? What are synonyms for discretion?
8. Characterize the humor of the Proverbs.
9. Can you find other examples of humor in this book?
10. Does the humor or irony have a serious purpose? Cite examples.

Chapter Ten

A STRING OF PEARLS

Have not I written unto thee excellent things
of counsels and knowledge,
To make thee know the certainty of the words of
truth,
That thou mayest carry back words of truth to
them that send thee?   Proverbs 22:20, 21

LOVERS OF POETRY, I have found, generally make a practice of marking favorite passages. This is the lover's way of claiming for himself particularly beautiful or expressive lines, and often he reads and repeats these chosen passages until they are committed, unconsciously, to memory. One of my chief pleasures is to call back to the consciousness snatches of poetry learned in grade school or high school. And if one finds an appropriate time and a willing listener or two, he can share these loved poems or lines and perhaps receive in return some of the lines that are significant to his friends.

Golden Apples

This practice of reciting what one likes evidently goes far back in man's history. Even in the Proverbs the beauty of certain expressions is carefully noted and praised:

A word fitly spoken
Is like apples of gold in a network of silver.
(25:11)

This passage, in itself, illustrates the truth that brevity and an appropriate figure can produce enduring beauty. Thus for ages this short couplet has been quoted to show that apt phrasing leaves a deep and pleasing impression. This little commentary on eloquence or force also illustrates a favorite device of the Hebrews: clothing an abstraction in clear, sharp, concrete terms and making the idea beautiful through use of appropriate figures. Here gold and silver, the most precious metals, are fashioned into apples (golden apples, beautiful words) and into a fine network (interlaced silver, the setting for the precious words).

A similar expression concerns good news. This passage has taken on great significance for missionaries serving far from home, and one of them years ago impressed the verse upon me by citing it in a letter:

> As cold waters to a thirsty soul,
> So is good news from a far country.
> (25:25)

Can one think of any figure more appropriate to express the gladness of the one far from home? Because the figure is so apt, and so well put, it is unforgettable.

Buy Up the Truth

Another succinct statement is like an epigram—sharp and to the point:

> Buy the truth and sell it not . . . (23:23)

The second line, in my judgment, could well be omitted, for it is lame in comparison to this forthright and practical command: it adds, by way of explanation, "Yea, wisdom, and instruction, and understanding"—the products that have been advertised and offered from chapter one onward. But no one can improve on the seven monosyllables which state a profound truth: when you find the truth, get it and keep it. Once again the language of concrete experience is used to state a great principle, and the result is powerful.

The choice of the word **buy** here is quite interesting. It is perhaps the first use of the expression so popular today: "I don't buy that." It is not likely that our modern usage came from the passage here quoted. Instead, the process of using a concrete, everyday term (this one from the marketplace) has been picked up and repeated. Since we buy all kinds of goods and gadgets, we have come to talk of "buying" proposals or ideas.

A Good Name

Reputation has been important in all ages. Today the popular expression, borrowed, no doubt, from the admen, is "image." Everybody, from the local undertaker to the president of the country, is concerned about his image. Often, it appears, public figures are more concerned about the image than about the reality. As Solomon expressed it,

> A good name is rather to be chosen than great riches,
> And loving favor than silver and gold.
>
> (22:1)

This can be called an expression of idealism. It stands in sharp contrast to the pragmatism of our age and to the practice of many public figures who prefer cash, or political favors, to a clean reputation. Experience has taught us that a man's reputation, over the years, comes to agree pretty well with the truth. A false reputation may stand for a time, but truth has a way of balancing the account.

Justice

Not far removed from this topic is the practice of justice. One of the excellent insights found in the Proverbs is this judgment:

> To do righteousness and justice
> Is more acceptable to Jehovah than sacrifice. (21:3)

This teaching is the message of the reforming prophets such as Amos and Hosea.

> For I desire goodness and not sacrifice; and the knowledge of God more than burnt-offerings. (Hosea 6:6)

> Yea, though ye offer me your burnt-offerings, and meal-offerings, I will not accept them; neither will I regard the peace-offerings of your fat beasts . . . But let justice roll down as waters, and righteousness as a mighty stream.
>
> (Amos 5:22, 24)

The passage in Proverbs is almost an echo of the words of the prophets. Their substance is almost identical. It may be hard to determine which came first—the verse in Proverbs or the statements in the prophets—but it is clear that this is a very high conception of man's ethical duty.

Righteousness and justice are judicial terms; they suggest equity and impartiality, giving to each person his just deserts. Kindness is a different kind of quality. It connotes more than fairness; it is gentleness, mercy, grace to one in need. I find deep truth in the assertion

That which maketh a man to be desired is his kindness . . . .
(19:22)

Men expect justice from a court of law, but they expect kindness from friends and family. Few qualities are more needed in social living than kindness, the generous thoughtfulness of those who express love in gentle words and little acts of affectionate regard. Wordsworth expressed the universal appreciation of kindliness in the famous lines:

". . . . or that best portion of a good man's life,
His little, nameless, unremembered acts of kindness and of love."

Another notable example of this rare quality is found in the description of the model wife and mother, the "worthy woman" described in the last book of Proverbs: "the law of kindness is on her tongue" (31:26b).

Where Love Is

Love, the highest and best quality of the human heart, also finds a place in the topics treated in this book. How true and forceful is this observation:

Better is a dinner of herbs, where love is,
Than a stalled ox and hatred therewith.
(15:17)

Such contrasts as this—love versus hatred—are made vivid by the reference to a very plain meal, enjoyed in an atmosphere of love, and a banquet accompanied by hatred. Thus, long ago, wise men saw that prosperity or even luxury does not bring happiness; that the relationships of persons, whether husbands and wives or employer and employees, far outweigh physical conditions. Perhaps the meal or dinner is chosen to illustrate the importance of attitude, since even the finest food may stick in the throat when anger or hatred prevails at the table. At a dinner the members of a family, or of an organized group, are drawn into a very close communion and the occasion which can and should be joyful can be spoiled by the coolness or criticism of some of the group (see also 17:1).

Many homes wisely avoid any discussion of troublesome matters at the dinner table. Probably most of us have been present at family meals when parents spent a good deal of the time upbraiding or criticizing the children, or the children quarreled with one another.

The dinner is spoiled, then, for everyone and one leaves the table depressed and unhappy. One little child, who had weathered some sharp criticism at the family table, was heard to remark, "Thou preparest a table before me in the presence of my enemies."

Another expression of the power of love is couched in an antithetic proverb:

Hatred stirreth up strifes;
But love covereth all transgressions.
(10:12)

The first half of this verse states an obvious truth, well known in ancient times as it is in ours. But the second line expresses a truth not fully understood or practiced until Christ came and showed the breadth and height and depth of love. Hatred naturally breeds hatred and produces strife. This process can go on almost unendingly unless someone has the moral strength to reverse the power of hate and show love when hate would be far more natural. (Some feuds have gone on so long that the latter generations did not know why they hated or killed members of the opposing clan: they were simply born to hate them.)

All of us know the power of a mother's or father's love. It can forgive the offending child, no matter how grave the wrong has been. This is possible because they are "disposed to" love, i.e., they want to love their own offspring. King David was able to love Absalom even when his son stole the hearts of David's subjects and revolted against his father. Paternal love was great enough to forgive the son's transgressions. Love, we learn from the beautiful analysis given by Paul, is longsuffering and kind, it is patient, it endures all things (even hatred and misrepresentation), and seeketh not its own advantage. Love provides the climate for fair and harmonious human relations; it is not deceitful or self-seeking. It is the motivation of true peacemakers. Like the love of God, it is freely given and seeks only to right the wrongs and bring harmony to discordant lives. The Apostle Peter admonished the believers to be "fervent in your love among yourselves; for love covereth a multitude of sins" (1 Peter 4:8).

The two passages—in Proverbs and in 1 Peter—agree that love is the one acceptable covering for sin. Pride or superiority is not a fit covering, for this means a smug and pharisaical attitude on the part of the forgiver. And since each of us, no matter how far we may have progressed spiritually, must continually ask forgiveness for wrongs we have done, we can only show love to our weak and faltering fellow sinners. By showing love to those who offend us, we are assured of God's mercy toward ourselves. Without this forgiving spirit, we are shut out from God's forgiveness (see Matt. 6:14, 15).

The Mastery of Self

Self-mastery or self-control is epitomized in this striking passage:

> He that is slow to anger is better than the mighty,
> And he that ruleth his spirit, than he that taketh a city.
>
> (16:32)

Two examples of power are mentioned here—the mighty man and the military conqueror. Homer's great warrior, Achilles, may serve to illustrate the anger of the mighty. Achilles was the most famous warrior of the Greeks in their war with the Trojans, but when Agamemnon, the Commander-in-chief of the Greek armies, took for himself a prize of war that had been given to Achilles and offered Achilles a similar but different prize, the great soldier retired from the battle and sulked in his tent. Various leaders tried in vain to get the warrior to return to the field, since without him the Greeks were being badly mauled, but he refused. His "honor" or pride had been offended. Not until his dearest friend, Patroclus, was killed by the Trojans could Achilles be persuaded to put on his armor again. Meantime, great numbers of the Greeks had been slain because Achilles had sulked like a spoiled child.

Another verse in Proverbs throws light on the passage about self-control:

> He that is slow to anger is of great understanding;
> But he that is hasty of spirit exalteth folly.
>
> (14:29)

The contrast between hot anger and a cool spirit is suggested in the statement that "he that is of a cool spirit is a man of understanding" (17:27). In these observations we see one of man's most prominent weaknesses—impatience or anger. Men of low and high intelligence, of good breeding and poor breeding, are often made ridiculous by their uncontrolled anger. Sometimes the anger is directed against a person but it may, quite irrationally, be directed against some object like a balky engine, or against a system such as the tax system or the military draft.

When one realizes that anger does not solve any problem but can radically reduce one's reasoning powers, the substitution of calmness for impatience and reason for angry behavior ought to be obvious. Anger may lead to irresponsible action and do great harm to anyone who happens to be near the raging man. So the seer reminds us that controlling oneself is more honorable than conquering a city.

A strong temper or anger is by no means undesirable, if it is kept under control. Anger is as natural as any other emotion, but, like fire, it must be carefully used or it can destroy property and persons. A man is less than a man when he is overcome by anger. He becomes more like a raging beast than a man. When anger gets out of control, it becomes a sin. This seems to be the meaning of Paul's statement, "Be ye angry and sin not . . ." (Eph. 4:26), which is translated in the New English Bible as "If you are angry, do not let anger lead you into sin." Phillips' paraphrase reads: "If you are angry, be sure that it is not out of wounded pride or bad temper."

Children must be taught early in life to control anger and to solve their problems calmly. Parents are responsible for teaching, correcting, and disciplining their own children, and fathers are specifically urged not to provoke anger or wrath in their children but to teach and train them to be obedient and self-controlled (Eph. 6:4). What difference is there between the wild tantrums of a spoiled child and the shocking display of uncontrolled anger in a man? Simply a matter of age. The adult has carried into middle age the unreasonable and disgusting behavior of a brat, but the child's action is more readily forgiven. "Let a bear robbed of her whelps meet a man, Rather than a fool in his folly" (17:12).

National Glory or Shame

On a higher level, since it concerns the fate of nations rather than of individuals, is this oft-quoted proverb:

> Righteousness exalteth a nation;
> But sin is a reproach to any people.
> (14:34)

Countless sermons have been preached from this favorite text, and it has often served statesmen as well. The thought of this verse is in reality the theme of the Old Testament. Again and again, in the Torah and the prophets, God called upon his chosen people to walk uprightly, to avoid the sins and idolatries of neighboring nations, and to seek justice and righteousness, both individually and nationally.

Rightly considered, the sentence in Proverbs ("Righteousness exalteth a nation, sin is a reproach to any people") is universal in its application. No reference is made here to Israel; rather all nations then and now are embraced in its judgment. The opposites expressed in this verse—righteousness as opposed to sin, and honor as opposed to reproach—is like a law of physics, applicable to all people.

In the "Recessional," written in 1897 to commemorate the Queen's Diamond Jubilee, when England was the greatest power on earth, Kipling called upon his countrymen to remember that their power was a trust from God and that humility rather than boastful pride should mark their achievements. The fourth stanza, like others, warns England:

> If, drunk with sight of power, we loose
> Wild tongues that have not Thee in awe,
> Such boastings as the Gentiles use,
> Or lesser breeds without the law:
> Lord God of hosts, be with us yet,
> Lest we forget, lest we forget.

Vision

Another loved and frequently quoted statement from the wisdom of the Proverbs is this:

> Where there is no vision, the people cast off restraint . . . .
> (29:18a)

The familiar King James Version says, "Where there is no vision, the people perish." In either reading, the primary emphasis falls on the first clause and particularly upon the term "vision." Traditionally many Americans have interpreted the word vision to mean farsightedness, forethought, long-range planning and have arrived, logically enough, at the conclusion: without such a view of matters, the people will perish. In other words, leadership or the farsighted plans of wise men have been considered essential to all progress, materially and spiritually. Though there may be truth in this understanding of the words, the actual text seems to have a quite different sense.

The Revised Standard Version reads, "Where there is no prophecy, the people cast off restraint." Various scholars take the position that the word translated "vision" or "prophecy" here means, indeed, the prophetic books included in the canon as the word "law" in the second stave refers to the Pentateuch. The Septuagint version translates the word "guide" or "interpreter" (see the *Interpreter's Bible,* Vol. 4). In a parallel passage (Proverbs 13:13) Israel is warned that

> Whoso despiseth the word bringeth destruction on himself;
> But he that feareth the commandment shall be rewarded.

Very likely the term "word" here means God's revelation made through the Law (Deut. 30:11-13).

Since the word "vision" is frequently used to mean God's word or will (see Amos 1:1 and Isaiah 1:1), the meaning in the verse under consideration is undoubtedly, "Without God's revealed will or prophecy, the people are doomed to perish." The passage might also be construed to mean, "Whoever disregards God's word does so at his own peril." Without Jehovah's guidance or leading, the people cast off all moral restraint or, as the original says, "let go." Thus it is not human leadership or vision that is set forth here as the basis for safety; it is, instead, God's revelation, which at that time was given through his prophets.

The Blessedness of Righteousness

Finally, there are several scattered passages which extol righteousness. The first of these is beautifully poetic:

> But the path of the righteous is as the dawning light
> That shineth more and more unto the perfect day.
>
> (4:18)

The second verse uses a figure from nature:

> The fruit of the righteous is a tree of life;
> And he that is wise winneth souls.
>
> (11:30)

The third one speaks of the earthly reward of the righteous:

> The memory of the righteous is blessed . . . .
>
> (10:7a)

The last one is also figurative:

> To the wise the way of life goeth upward.
> That he may depart from Sheol beneath.
>
> (15:24)

In all these verses the righteous or faithful man is pictured as pleasing God and receiving his blessing. The first one compares the life of the righteous to the dawning light, the soft, rose-tinted light of breaking day. At dawn the light is scattered and weak, but as the sun climbs, the light grows clearer and stronger. So too does the life and influence of the godly person. As god's great luminary moves higher and higher, the day continues to grow brighter, and in the same way the path of the righteous climbs higher each day. God's people are quite naturally called "children of the day," just as Satan's followers are "children of darkness" or of disobedience. And as the sun brings light and warmth to the earth, so do Christians bring light, truth, and love to a dark and troubled world. The Christian's task is to be true to the divine call: "that ye may become blameless and harmless, children of God without blemish in the midst of a crooked and perverse generation, among whom ye are seen as lights in the world" (Phil. 2:15). The believer is to keep moving toward "the perfect day," the time of his final redemption.

A Tree of Life

The second passage speaks of the fruitage of a righteous life; the wise and faithful believer winneth souls. The choice of the metaphor here (a "tree of life") indicates God's purpose for the redeemed, that is, to bear believers or win souls for Christ. Just as each tree, since time began, brings forth after its own kind, so faith produces faith and conviction, conviction. Happily, one tree can bear an unbelievable harvest, and each seed it drops can in due time produce hundreds or thousands more of its kind. So a good life brings forth good fruit, which in turn produces more. In the same way evil produces itself and keeps the cycle going.

A tribute to the good life of righteous persons is found in the words "The memory of the righteous is blessed."

It seems characteristic of all right-thinking and normal people to desire a good reputation, and this craving seems to grow stronger as we near the end of life on earth. The letters, diaries, conversations, and printed words of multitudes bear witness to the fact that people want to be remembered in a favorable light. Even suicides often leave papers which they hope will clear their names and perhaps gain for them a fair reputation. Philanthropists leave large sums of money to establish hospitals, schools, libraries, orphanages, hoping thereby to influence the world for good after they are gone and, perhaps, to keep alive their memory at least for a little time on earth. Poets and playwrights, artists and artisans, seek through their works to perpetuate their names. At the same time, other poets and philosophers point out how vain are these earthly strivings for immortality. Perhaps the best monument possible to anyone on earth is to be remembered with love by a great many persons. Something of the faith, zeal or fervency of such lives passes into others and continues to influence others beyond man's power to measure. The highest goal of a good life may be to leave such an influence as this.

Finally, "to the wise the way of life goeth upward." To the evolutionist this has a very definite but physical meaning. To the person who understands the slow and painful struggle of man to overcome the pull of the flesh and to rise, ever so slowly, toward the high mark God has set for his children, it means the victory of faith. We begin as physical beings. For a long time we are not even aware of the spirit within us, but when this awareness comes and we are committed to the spiritual rather than the carnal life, we begin to grow.

Questions

1. This chapter deals with a variety of topics, each one resembling a flawless pearl. Name some of the principal topics.
2. How can one "buy the truth"? Why should he not sell it?
3. Why is a good reputation to be cherished?
4. Are reputation and character necessarily distinct? How are they related?
5. How do you define righteousness? How do the prophets define it?
6. Discuss the value of love—in the family circle, in the larger community.
7. Discuss the appropriateness of the figure of speech calling the righteous person "a tree of life."

Chapter Eleven

THE JOY AND CROWN OF AGE

"Children's children are the crown of old men." Proverbs 17:6

LITERATURE ABOUNDS in tributes to children. Quite often it is the sweetness, innocence, or trustfulness of children that is celebrated in a lyric or a fine passage of prose. In the Psalms occurs a brief song of ascents attributed to Solomon, a part of which follows:

Lo, children are a heritage of Jehovah;
And the fruit of the womb is his reward.
As arrows in the hand of a might man,
So are the children of youth.
Happy is the man that hath his quiver full of them . . . .
(Psalm 127:3-5)

A moving tribute to children born in one's later years is this passage from Wordsworth's poem *Michael,* the story of a kind old shepherd to whom a child is given late in life:

. . . . but to Michael's heart
This son of his old age was yet more dear—
Less from instinctive tenderness, the same
Fond spirit that blindly works in the blood of all—
Than that a child, more than all other gifts
That earth can offer to declining man,
Brings hope with it, and forward-looking thoughts.

Both the Old and New Testaments place a high value upon children and childlike qualities. Many of the famous stories of the Bible concern children: the birth of Moses, the childhood and early manhood of Joseph, the boy Samuel, young David's exploits, Daniel and his three Hebrew friends in bondage, the birth of John the

84

Baptist, the annunciation and birth of Jesus, as well as the many occasions when Jesus received and blessed little children. More than once Jesus chose a little child to illustrate the principles required of his disciples—humility, a trusting faith, gentleness, and teachableness. Both the prophets of the Old Testament and the writers of the New show deep respect and love for children and emphasize repeatedly that children should be taught to reverence God and his word.

What the Child Brings to a Home

Many passages of Scripture make clear the joy and blessing of having children. When Eve conceived and bore Cain, her first-born, she said, "I have gotten a man with the help of Jehovah." One recalls, also, the cry of the barren Rachel, "Give me children, or else I die" (Genesis 30:1) and the deep longing of Hannah for a child—and her love for the child that God gave her. (1 Sam. 1; cf. Psalm 113:9). In Psalm 128 God declares that his blessing will rest on the faithful:

> Thy wife shall be as a fruitful vine,
> In the innermost parts of thy house;
> Thy children like olive plants,
> Round about thy table.

A child comes into the world without any taint of evil (no matter how its parents may have lived), without personality, knowledge, prejudice, or antagonisms. Its mind, yet undeveloped, is, in the eighteenth century phrase, a *tabula rasa*, a tablet without writing. But from its very first experiences the child begins to learn and to change. It is the child's capacity to grow and develop—physically, mentally, socially—that makes the experience of child-rearing so challenging, so dangerous, and so rewarding. Although each child is born with latent tendencies and certain characteristics (such as a strong will), it has no evil (inherited or learned) and no inborn prejudices. Its loves and fears, as well as its language and antagonisms, will be learned from those around it. Parents, in their molding the mind and disposition of the child, are thus co-workers with God in the "making of man."

> We are all blind until we see
>   That in the human plan,
> Nothing is worth the making
>   That does not make the man.

Edwin Markham

85

What We Owe Our Children

Thoughtful parents begin planning for the birth of a child long before the child is expected. In addition to planning the physical environment for the baby, they prepare themselves—and the children in the family, if there are older children, for the coming of the new member. The birth of a child is an event of great importance, and couples who want children and are qualified to care for and train them, make many plans and adjustments before the baby arrives.

One of the differences between a good home and an unfit home for children is the atmosphere that prevails. In the home of a loving and well-adjusted couple, there will be warmth, trust, a freedom from tension and quarreling, a sense of security and stability. In such an atmosphere, parents, children, relatives, and visitors can be comfortable, relaxed, and natural. Every child deserves, but unfortunately, does not get, such a home as its birthright. In the happy home, children are normally cheerful, eager to take part in all activities, and they have a strong though unconscious sense of belonging.

The home as God intended it will have two devoted parents, each concerned about the other's welfare and both deeply devoted to the child's growth and development as a healthy, happy, well-adjusted member of the family. The parents—ideally—will be agreed on what they consider best for the child or children, on what behavior is "right" or "wrong" for the child, and how discipline or control should be handled. They will be aware of the harm that quarreling and fault-finding with each other can have on the children, whether the children are quite young or teenagers. The parents should know that they determine the atmosphere of the home and that their attitudes have a profound influence on the child's views and personality.

Importance of Discipline

One of the evidences of real affection in the home is discipline or training—a subject given considerable attention in Proverbs. It is possible that discipline in former times was often too authoritarian and severe. Many who are past the meridian of life can remember hearing the old expression "Children are to be seen and not heard!" Fortunately, this generation has rejected that absurd idea. But in swinging away from the old autocratic rule, where the father laid down the law and everyone ran for cover, many families have swung to the opposite extreme of permissiveness. In some homes children now say what they will or will not do, and the parents surrender without even a battle.

Good discipline begins quite early in the child's life—as soon as he can understand what the parents mean—and continues until the young man or young woman is mature enough to make responsible decisions and carry them out. Proper discipline is intended to teach the growing child what is socially approved or disapproved, and it is effected by various kinds of rewards and punishments. With the small child, a pat or a kiss or even a wide smile of approval can be a satisfying reward. Older children can be rewarded with privileges as well as words of appreciation.

Discipline involves the teaching of obedience, of respect for older persons, and respect for the rights and feelings of others. It is general knowledge that a small child is totally self-centered and, if allowed always to have his own way, soon becomes a young tyrant. By slow degrees the parents must teach it to recognize the claims of other children for attention, the rights of others to express themselves or play with his toys, and the need for self-control. Unless the child learns early in life to respect authority and to obey those placed over him, he will learn later in life "that the way of the transgressor is hard" (Prov. 13:15). Parents who fail to teach these basic principles of behavior are making their child a rebellious, disdainful, and unhappy person.

Some First Principles of Child Training

One of the best-known passages in Proverbs, and one frequently quoted if not followed is this:

> Train up a child in the way he should go,
> And even when he is old he will not depart from it.
> (22:6)

The training of a child begins in infancy as the parents respond to the child's needs, and give it attention, love, and care. At each stage of the infant's development, it learns new skills and responds to new stimuli—sounds, colors, shapes, and the spoken word. Long before the child can speak, it can understand the meaning of affection and even of certain words. Most parents begin teaching the meaning of "no" as soon as the child can crawl and begin his exploration of tables, drawers, and other things within reach. Any teaching which is to be effective must be suited to the child's age, must be regular, consistent, and clear in intention.

A key word in the passage noted earlier is "train." This means far more than telling, showing, or punishing. The statement in Proverbs 22:6 gives both a principle and a promise: The principle is: train the child, regularly, faithfully, consistently; and the promise is "he will not depart from it." To train (a term derived ultimately from the Latin verb *trahere,* to draw or lead) means to instruct, to guide, educate, discipline, and correct. It necessitates love and care, almost endless patience, and the repetition of the skill or knowledge to be mastered until the desired response is almost automatic. A nurseryman or gardener knows the patience—and the rewards— of training a plant or shrub to follow a trellis or a pattern he has planned. Those who train pets or wild animals tell us that patience, persistence, firmness, and kindness are all needed—with infinite practice—to gain the desired ends.

The teaching of Proverbs on child-rearing is supplemented by some passages in the New Testament. One of these is a statement found in Ephesians:

> Children, obey your parents in the Lord: for this is right. Honor thy father and mother (which is the first commandment with promise), that it may be well with thee, and thou mayest live long on the earth.
>
> Ephesians 6:1-3

To whom was this teaching of Paul's directed, to children or to parents? Obviously, doctors and psychologists, as well as Christian teachers, give direction to *parents* for the benefit of children. What child will learn to obey unless he is taught? Is obedience learned from association with other children—or at school? Too often this teaching is left to the school or to society, and the uncorrected child suffers for the want of proper home training. One more question: Will the child naturally honor his mother and father if he has grown up like a plant, without nurture or training? Obedience and gratitude are both the products of good teaching, the lack of which can embitter the child's life and affect his relations with schoolmates, friends, and his marriage partner later in life.

Is the Bible teaching on discipline too severe? Is it no longer valid because of the findings of modern psychology? A great many thinkers and educators do not believe so. Obviously there are extremes to be avoided. Occasionally parents will beat a child unmercifully (studies show such parents are often abnormal or even psychotic), but the opposite extreme of permissiveness and virtually no control is probably much more common in America. Each of these extremes can be quite harmful to the child and can affect adversely his social adjustment.

To return to the Proverbs, several other scriptures support the doctrine that correcting children is a sign of love by the parents:

> The rod and reproof give wisdom;
> But a child left to himself causeth shame to his mother.
>
> (29:15)

> Correct thy son, and he will give thee rest;
> Yea, he will give delight unto thy soul.
>
> (29:17)

> Chasten thy son, seeing there is hope;
> And set not thy heart on his destruction.
>
> (19:18)

> My son, be wise, and make my heart glad,
> That I may answer him that reproacheth me.
>
> (27:11)

Such passages make clear that the fruit of right training is shown in the behavior of the child: "he will give thee rest," "he will give delight unto thy soul." Truly, the child that has been well trained is a confident, strong, and agreeable person; whereas the child that went uncorrected becomes a problem to himself and a nuisance to his neighbors. Some law enforcement officers say that a young person who flouts the law has never had the word "no" explained to him in terms that he can understand!

Perhaps, even in Solomon's day, some children would not accept discipline and so had to bear the penalty later. This is suggested strongly by such observations as these:

> He that being often reproved hardeneth his neck
> Shall suddenly be destroyed, and that without remedy.
>
> (29:1)

> A servant will not be corrected by words;
> For though he understand, he will not give heed.
>
> (29:19)

> There is a generation that curse their father,
> And bless not their mother.
> There is a generation that are pure in their own eyes,
> And yet are not washed from their filthiness.
> There is a generation, oh how lofty are their eyes!
> And their eyelids are lifted up.
>
> (30:11-13)

It would be unfair to end this discussion on a pessimistic note. Put in the simplest terms, we may say that good parents have good children, and the finest homes in turn produce good children and happy homes. The reverse is likewise true, *for like produces like,* whether in crops, or calves, or children.

Some Rewards

There are many rewards in having children. They give an added dimension to life. We live again in our children and grandchildren, sharing their achievements, their problems, their hopes and joys. In them we also find fulfillment of many of our best dreams. To watch a child grow from helpless babyhood to a man or woman filling a responsible position in life, perhaps leading, teaching, or serving humanity in other important ways is one of life's greatest joys. And for Christian parents, one of the highest rewards of parenthood is to see their children establish faithful Christian homes where God's word is reverenced and children are brought up in the atmosphere of love and wholesome respect for one another and for what is right.

More honor should be given to those who rear children that become a blessing to society—the mothers and fathers of ministers, nurses, physicians, missionaries, Christian leaders, educators, and all whose lives inspire or help to lift the lives of their fellowmen. Young people can show the way by honoring their own deserving parents in ways to show gratitude.

Questions

1. Name some qualities of children extolled in the Scriptures.
2. What gifts does a child bring to a home where it is wanted?
3. In what way do parents share with God in the creation and shaping of life?
4. What, besides normal care, do we owe our children?
5. Explain the meaning of sharing oneself with a child.
6. What is the basic meaning of discipline? Discuss its application to children.
7. Why are children happier under reasonable restraint?
8. Enumerate some important biblical principles on training children.
9. Does the teaching of Proverbs on the subject of discipline seem too harsh?
10. Comment on the axiom: "Like produces like."
11. Are children worth the trouble and expense they entail?

Chapter Twelve

THE POWER OF THE TONGUE

Whoso keepeth his mouth and his tongue
Keepeth his soul from troubles.
Proverbs 21:23

Death and life are in the power of the tongue.
Proverbs 18:21

NO OTHER BOOK, to my knowledge, deals so fully and emphatically with the power of words—both for good and evil—as the Proverbs. Speech in all of its tones and intentions is here held up to the light. And, in characteristic fashion, this book deals with the subject directly, pointedly, and practically. The right use of language is praised, the wrong uses condemned, and the empty and foolish phrases reproved.

Words are of great value and interest, not only for what they say but also because of what they reveal about the speaker. If we listen long enough we can determine, to some degree at least, how bold or shy one is, how skilled he is in language, how he sees himself and others, and whether he "weighs his words" or uses them recklessly.

Because words, like fire or dynamite, have such a great potential for creating or destroying, they must be used with care. With words we win friends or alienate persons, inspire faith or create doubt, encourage the faint-hearted or preach defeat.

With simple words marriages are formed or, in far too many instances, dissolved. With words of truth and conviction, ministers lead scores of men and women to accept Christ's way. With words of soberness, legislators debate the issues that will shape many thousands of lives. Sometimes, hasty and thoughtless words destroy friendships or drive persons out of the church. Rulers and judges have the power to sentence men to death or to revoke their sentences—with a half dozen words. It is almost impossible to determine the potential of words for either blessing or hurting others.

STUDIES IN PROVERBS
Words of Wisdom

Proverbs begins with a brief discourse on the purpose and value of religious instruction:

> To know wisdom and instruction;
> To discern the words of understanding;
> To receive instruction in wise dealing,
> In righteousness and justice and equity.
> (1:2-3)

In declaring openly that the aim of the work is to teach wise living, understanding of God's will and fair treatment of all persons, high or low, it is clear that the writers are undertaking not only to teach but to influence conduct. Instruction in righteousness—that is, the right way to live happily and righteously—is the declared aim of the book. (Note also Prov. 1:23-26; 4:1-10, 20-23; 5:1-7). The tone in all these passages is one of deep concern, as of a father pleading with the son he loves (see 2:1; 3:1-4; 4:1-4). Two qualities in particular are stressed: wisdom, or full knowledge and understanding; and righteousness, or right conduct. "Wisdom is the principal thing; therefore, get wisdom" (4:7). Again, "For Jehovah giveth wisdom; out of his mouth cometh wisdom and understanding" (2:6). As a result, "Then shalt thou understand righteousness and justice, and equity, yea, every good path." Knowledge is the light and righteousness is the path.

Words of Encouragement

In chapter 8 wisdom is personified. She stands on the high places and "where the paths meet," calling to men to forsake folly, pride, and lying.

> Hear, for I will speak excellent things;
> And the opening of my lips shall be right things . . .
> There is nothing crooked or perverse in them.
> They are all plain to him that understandeth.
> (8:6; 8, 9)

Wholesome speech is the medium of instruction. There is good psychology in the saying,

> The wise in heart will receive commandments,
> But a prating fool shall fall.
> (10:8)

92

Then in a beautiful figure of speech the writer adds,

The mouth of the righteous is a fountain of life (10:11).

A fountain flows because it is fed from springs deep within the earth. The truly righteous person draws his inner strength not from any self-generated righteousness but from the power which God supplies. It is that spring of living water which Christ promised to those who do his will (John 4:14).

> The fruit of the righteous is a tree of life,
> And he that is wise winneth souls.
> (11:30)

Here the power of righteousness continues, like a fruitful tree, to produce good fruit year after year, and *this* fruit is souls redeemed from sin and brought to God. Each Christian should be inspired by this wonderful power of growth, usefulness, and the influence that can win souls for Christ.

The contrast between wisdom and human folly is stated clearly in these words:

> He that uttereth truth showeth forth righteousness;
> But a false witness, deceit.
> (12:17)
> The lip of truth shall be established forever;
> But a lying tongue is but for a moment.
> (12:19)

True words stand, like God's own promises, forever; but lies, in personal relations or in national affairs, are soon exposed and last only "for a moment." Truth has nothing to fear, lies shrink from the light and die in ignominy. Therefore, the wise person—whether a youth, a parent, a governor, or president—will avoid the temptation to gain a momentary advantage by lies and deception.

Whoever would enjoy a reputation for truth and integrity and be remembered as a friend and benefactor of his people must learn to control the most dangerous member, the oily and slippery tongue (compare James 3:2-5).

Wrong Uses of the Tongue

Many warnings are given in Proverbs about the snares of the scarlet woman:

Behold, there met him a woman
With the attire of a harlot, and wily of heart.
She is clamorous and wilful;
Her feet abide not in her house . . .
So she caught him and kissed him,
And with an impudent face she [enticed him].
(7:10, 11; 13)

She is described as "the foreigner that flattereth with her words"(7:5) and wins the "young man void of understanding" (7:7).

With her much fair speech she causeth him to yield;
With the flattering of her lips she forceth him
along . . . As an ox to the slaughter.
(7:21, 22)
For the lips of a strange woman drop honey,
And her mouth is smoother than oil.
(5:3)

Notable in these passages is the persuasiveness of the harlot; with her tongue she seduces the simple ones and makes the affair seem innocent and natural. Because she makes evil so attractive, chapters five, six, and seven offer many admonitions and warnings to the young.

The Loose Tongue

Whispering and backbiting are two of the common wrongs in community life:

A worthless person . . . is he that walketh with a
    perverse mouth . . .
Who deviseth evil continually
Who soweth discord.
(6:12, 14)
With his mouth the godless man destroyeth his neighbor.
(11:9)
He that goeth about as a talebearer revealeth secrets;
Therefore company not with him that openeth wide his lips.
(20:19)
A perverse man scattereth abroad strife;
And a whisperer separateth chief friends.
(16:28)

Irresponsible talk—whispering, backbiting, gossiping—can do irreparable harm. It is like a fire out of control, or like a wind that scatters trash and debris over a city. And loose talk can sow discord even among friends or, as the writer declares, "destroy" a neighbor. Such talk is a deadly evil; no self-respecting person will engage in it or encourage it. Well did the ancient writer say, "the mouth of the wicked poureth out evil things" (15:28).

A similar problem is the continued "harping on the matter" which, likewise, "separateth chief friends" (17:9). This kind of harping has nothing to do with heaven; it creates its own hell.

One other incredible sin is mentioned as evidence of a perverse and evil heart:

> There is a generation that curse their father,
> And bless not their mother.
>
> (30:11)

The Mosaic law discouraged this kind of behavior by saying that such a degenerate "shall surely be put to death" (Exodus 21:17)

The Deliberate Lie

In the eyes of many there are two kinds of lies—little, harmless lies, social affairs—and the real lies, designed to cover one's tracks or to make some other person the goat. But in the Scripture, lies do not come in several colors. A lie is evil because its purpose is to deceive or gain an advantage; it deliberately falsifies and misleads, usually for highly personal reasons. Since God cannot tolerate lies or liars (Rev. 22:15), every kind of lie, whether in business, politics or even religion, is an abomination to him. In the catalogue of sins "hateful to God," three concern the misuse of the tongue:

> Haughty eyes, a lying tongue . . .
> A false witness that uttereth lies,
> And he that soweth discord among brethren.
>
> (6:17, 19)
>
> Be not a witness against thy neighbor without cause;
> And deceive not with thy lips.
>
> (24:28)

The Right Uses of Speech

Though a great part of the teaching in Proverbs is negative, warning against various kinds of wrong conduct, there are also many striking examples of positive and wholesome advice. And these principles are as valid today as when they first were uttered. Here are examples of sound teaching:

A soft answer turneth away wrath;
But a grievous word stirreth up anger.
The tongue of the wise uttereth knowledge aright . . .
(15:1-2)
Pleasant words are as a honeycomb,
Sweet to the soul, and health to the bones
(16:24).
He that spareth his words hath knowledge;
And he that is of a cool spirit is a man of
understanding.
(17:27)
Hear counsel and receive instruction,
That thou mayest be wise in the latter end.
(19:20)
(As we grow older we should grow wiser—HW.)

Whoso keepeth his mouth and his tongue
Keepeth his soul from troubles.
(21:23)

Some Final Words

Since, as we have seen, words have the power to arouse, to anger, to disturb and unsettle individuals or whole communities, every serious and thoughtful person should use words sparingly and responsibly. Christians especially need to be most careful in the use of the tongue. A foolish or suggestive remark can be picked up and carried about to the great detriment of the speaker, for "the simple believeth every word" (14:15). Each of us should remember, "God is in heaven and thou upon the earth; therefore let thy words be few" (Eccles. 5:2b). And we are reminded, also, that men must give account of their words in the day of judgment (Matt. 12:36). This explains why "death and life are in the power of the tongue" (18:21).

As one abiding principle we should always speak the truth, fully and fairly. "Wherefore, putting away falsehood, speak ye truth each one with his neighbor . . . ." (Eph. 4:25). Proverbs is also quite explicit: "He that rebuketh a man shall afterward find more favor than he that flattereth with his tongue" (28:23). Paul was happy to say that he "shrank not from declaring to you the whole counsel of God" (Acts 20:27).

In our relations with others we are taught to be fair and reasonable:

> Debate thy cause with thy neighbor himself,
> And disclose not the secret of another.
>
> (25:9)

The person who strives to be reasonable in all things will promote peace and understanding. He will "seek peace and pursue it." Again we read:

> It is an honor for a man to keep aloof from strife;
> But every fool will be quarreling.
>
> (20:3)

If misunderstandings do occur, and they will, the wise person keeps his voice down and his tongue under control. Here the "soft answer"—i.e., not incindiary words or tones—will usually prevent an angry confrontation. We must remember the old adage, "It takes two to quarrel."

Questions

1. Why is speech one of the best indexes of character?
2. Is it possible to control another person's speech? Can one control his own tongue? How?
3. What is one of the conditions (cited in 1 Peter 3:10) for enjoying life and good relations with others?
4. Name some of the beneficial uses of speech—in the home, in personal relations, in the church of God.
5. In what respect is the tongue like a fire? (example: Prov. 26:20).
6. Cite some of the warnings about the misuse of the tongue.
7. What positive admonitions are given in Proverbs concerning the right use of the tongue?
8. How do you interpret the sentence, "A man is tried by his praise," (Prov. 27:21). Consider what or whom he praises, and how he praises (half-heartedly, grudgingly, with enthusiasm).

Chapter Thirteen

AN IDEAL WIFE AND MOTHER

A worthy woman who can find?
For her price is far above rubies.
The heart of her husband trusteth in her,
And he shall have no lack of gain.
Proverbs 31:10, 11

PROBABLY NO OTHER portrait in all literature has depicted so clearly and lovingly the qualities of a good woman as the passage on ideal womahood which concludes the last chapter of the Proverbs. For nearly three thousand years, multiplied generations of Jewish and Christian families have found both inspiration and a model of womanly perfection in this famous passage.

Mothers in ancient Israel undoubtedly used this description of a virtuous woman to teach their daughters the tasks as well as the graces of a faithful and loving wife and mother. And, in the same way, those mothers must have instructed their sons in the kind of woman to choose for a wife. This, at least, is strongly implied by the fact that Lemuel, who learned these words from his own mother, is credited with preserving this "oracle" or teaching (see the opening words of Proverbs 31).

In Christian congregations this description of the ideal woman has been used on innumerable occasions as the basis for sermons on Mother's Day or for funerals, as well as for lessons pointing out the qualities and duties of married women. It has often been read as a fitting memorial for a truly good woman who lived unselfishly for her family and for others. What other tribute, in sacred or secular literature, can match this passage in beauty or feeling? It stands without peer.

A Timeless Picture

One of the reasons for the universal appeal of this prose poem is that the description is timeless. It described quite accurately the activities and the ideals of a matron in the time of Solomon; it applies in almost every detail to a woman of the twentieth century who has the care of a home and children and yet finds time for outside activities. Only one or two of the tasks named here (providing fuel for the lamps and laying "her hands to the distaff") do not apply to modern women, but up to the close of the nineteenth century even these details were appropriate to the life of women in the western world.

Yet in some respects this portrait is quite typical of the twentieth-century American housewife who, like her ancient prototype, engages in business. "She considereth a field and buyeth it" (vs. 16) and "She maketh linen garments and selleth them" (vs. 24) and takes time to help the unfortunate ("She stretcheth out her hand to the poor" (vs. 20). What could be more fitting than this description of a wife who, in addition to household duties, participates in the business and social life of the community?

The ideal woman, even in the ancient time, was not merely a homebody who spent all her waking hours cooking, sewing, and mending. Certainly the emphasis in this poem is the home life of the woman, but her life is not confined to the home. Other interests have their rightful place, too.

A Representative Woman

Another reason why this passage has been so universally loved is that the woman described here can be anyone's mother. There is no reference to suggest one race or another, nor any national peculiarities. In this respect the portrait is superior to any painting or sculpture of a fine or distinguished woman, for these art forms would almost certainly have traces of racial or national characteristics. Quite appropriately, the choice of language here *universalizes* the subject and makes her the ideal for any race or religion.

Does the question that opens this fine passage—"A worthy woman who can find?"—suggest that the writer was a cynic? The tone of the whole poem negates this idea. Instead, the thought seems to be that such a woman is like a rare jewel—to be sought and prized. In another chapter we read "A worthy woman is the crown of her husband" (12:4) and another reference suggests that a faithful wife is a gift from God:

Houses and riches are an inheritance from fathers;
But a prudent wife is from Jehovah.
(19:14)

"Whoso findeth a wife findeth a good thing," the writer declared, "and obtaineth favor of Jehovah" (18:22).

The subject of wives, like other topics in the book of Proverbs, is presented in contrasts. Consider the following statements:

Every wise woman buildeth her house;
But the foolish plucketh it down with her own hands.
(14:1)

As a ring in a swine's snout,
So is a fair woman that is without discretion.
(11:22)

It is better to dwell in the corner of the housetop,
Than with a contentious woman in a wide house.
(25:24)

Thus careless, contentious, and wicked women are contrasted with the virtuous, hard-working, and prudent wife depicted in chapter thirty-one. By implication the good wife is also presented as the opposite of the courtesans or "strange women" described in the early chapters of this book.

She Can Be Trusted

The first characteristic of the worthy woman is her trustworthiness: "The heart of her husband trusteth in her." To the woman who shares his life the husband trusts his property, his good name, and his children. He can safely give anything he has to her and know that it is safe, for her life is fulfilled in her home and marriage.

She doeth him good and not evil
All the days of her life.
(31:12)

And near the close of the poem the children and husband praise the queen of the home for her blessed influence on their lives. This passage will be noted later.

She is an industrious woman, who rises early and works willingly:

She seeketh wool and flax
And worketh willingly with her hands.
She is like the merchant ships;
She bringeth her bread from afar.
She riseth also while it is yet night,

And giveth food to her household,
And their task to her maidens.
(31:13-15)

In addition to her own work, she supervises the work of her household. A wise mother will not do all the work for her children, even though some have mistakenly done this under the prompting of love, for she knows that her children must be trained to care for themselves and assume their part of the household work. Where can self-reliance and the many responsibilities of family life be taught better than in the home, beginning in one's early years? And to the mother falls the chief responsibility for teaching the children these primary lessons in caring for themselves and sharing the work.

Our First Teachers

The mother has in all ages been the first teacher. From her the child learns the meaning of approval (of "yes" and "no"), of obedience, of helping and sharing. On another level the child learns its language from her; thus we speak correctly of the "mother tongue." Her words and accents leave a lasting impression on the child's mind, and her love and care go a long way toward shaping the personality of the child. So, unconsciously, the child learns lessons of trust, obedience, kindliness, and sympathy in a good home.

Mothers have been the first teachers of religion. Their unselfish love becomes for the child, at a later time, a symbol of God's love and care. The lessons they teach in obedience and responsibility prepare the child to do what he is told to do and thus to live in harmony with others. In addition, many mothers have taught their children simple prayers at bedtime and the habit of saying thanks at meals. Going beyond these early attempts to make the child God-conscious, religious families have often made it a practice to read a Bible story to the children at some regular time, thus adding to the atmosphere of Christian love and concern the values of direct teaching from the Bible. Many of the eminent writers of the past have mentioned the influence of Bible reading and prayers in the home as having an important influence in shaping both their ideals and their language.

Unselfish Living

The true mother, the ideal depicted in Proverbs, lives for others. Her children, her husband, her neighbors, and even "the needy" are blessed by her thoughtfulness.

She perceiveth that her merchandise is profitable;
Her lamp goeth not out by night.

(31:18)

She stretcheth out her hand to the poor;
Yea, she reacheth forth her hands to the needy.

(31:20)

She is not afraid of the snow for her household;
For all her household are clothed with scarlet.

(31:21)

Three qualities of character are evident in these verses: first, the good wife's careful provisions for her family; second, her compassion (the poor are not forgotten in her primary concern for her own circle); and third, her farsightedness in making warm clothing for all members of the household.

But in her dedication to others this mother does not neglect herself and become a drab and listless person.

She maketh for herself carpets of tapestry;
Her clothing is fine linen and purple.

(31:22)

Then, after beautifying her home and dressing herself attractively, "She maketh linen garments and selleth them." Through her ceaseless activity she became an ideal of the busy, and later of the business, woman—industrious, thrifty, and efficient.

From the description of the garments made by her hands, it is but a step to the figurative language which follows:

Strength and dignity are her clothing;
And she laugheth at the time to come.

(31:25)

Here are three more admirable traits of character: strength, dignity, and confidence. She is a self-reliant and courageous woman; conscious of her place in life and filling it with joy. Just as our grandmothers canned fruits and vegetables in the time of harvest to provide for the family's later needs, this model wife went about her tasks confidently and joyfully.

A Mother's Reward

The poem is rising to a climax as it moves from the strength and bearing of this heroic woman to a description of her personality, again expressed in richly poetic language:

She openeth her mouth with wisdom;
And the law of kindness is on her tongue.

(31:25)

Here, apparently, the writer is paying his subject two of the highest compliments: her speech (as well as her life) is filled with wisdom—one of the attributes of God and of all who love his will—and her tongue is controlled by the beautiful virtue of kindness.

How appropriately the quality of wisdom, which was extolled at length in the opening part of this book, should be personified in the final chapter in the behavior of this ideal person. Wisdom, of course, embraces good judgment, discretion, understanding, and highmindedness; it has been called repeatedly "the principal thing," and it comes from a knowledge of God. Here we see wisdom in the purest and best of God's creatures—a virtuous woman.

Yet this wisdom, with all its powers, would not be attractive or feminine were it lacking in kindness. Strength, whether of body or mind, can be arrogant and cruel. Wit, for example, is the playfulness of a keen mind, but quite often it is egotistical and cutting. A brilliant woman is quite often spoiled by adulation, and such a person frequently finds pleasure in sardonic remarks.

A truly gracious person carefully avoids hurting others, and of the qualities which make a woman lovable none can be compared to kindness. This gentleness seeks to make others feel at ease, it is given spontaneously to the shy or self-conscious, it smoothes over the *faux pas* or breach of good manners with a smile and word of compassion. More than any other quality, kindness makes a woman quick to understand another's need and to offer encouragement and confidence.

The high point of this descriptive poem is reached in the tribute of the woman's family:

> Her children rise up and call her blessed;
> And her husband also, and he praiseth her, saying
> Many daughters have done worthily,
> But thous excellest them all.
>
> (31:28, 29)

This passage can rightly be called the climax because it turns from a factual commentary on the woman's life and work to the words of deep appreciation spoken by her own children and husband. The children bless her for her goodness expressed in countless acts of kindness and love; and the husband—justly proud of one who has brought him so much happiness and fulfillment—praises his wife as having excelled all other women.

After the joyous climax, when the good woman has been given the praise due to her by those who love her most, the poem adds only a few concluding thoughts.

Grace is deceitful, and beauty is vain;
But a woman that feareth Jehovah, she shall be praised.
Give her of the fruit of her hands;
And let her works praise her in the gates.

(31:30, 31)

This passage contrasts physical beauty, which inevitably fades away, with the inner and lasting beauty of a consecrated life. It calls attention once more to the ideal of godly wisdom and the results of such wisdom in shaping a beautiful character.

What is the reward for a faithful life? The answer given here is that it is "the fruit of her hands," the enjoyment of her long, unselfish labors. By giving love to others, she receives love in full measure. By living for her husband and children, she now lives, to a great degree, in their lives and achievements.

Give her of the fruit of her hands,
And let her works praise her in the gates.

She enjoys a well-earned reputation for good deeds, for a fine family, and for a successful husband, "who is known in the gates, when he sitteth among the elders of the land." A good name and a good family are two of life's best rewards.

Questions

1. Cite some reasons for the appreciation in which this portrait is held.
2. In what respect is this picture timeless and universal?
3. Discuss the variety of activities of this woman, both in and out of the home.
4. List and comment on the chief characteristics of the "worthy woman."
5. Show the importance of mothers as teachers.
6. How does the good woman show her wisdom and grace in speech?
7. What is the climax of this tribute? Can you conceive of a higher tribute?
8. Note how husband, children, and community show gratitude for the faithful wife's life and works.